# QUALITY ASSURANCE IN REHABILITATION NURSING

## A PRACTICAL GUIDE

**Adrianne E. Avillion, MS, RN, CRRN, CNA**
Rehabilitation Staff Development Specialist
Montebello Rehabilitation Hospital
Baltimore, Maryland

**Barbara B. Mirgon, BSN, RN, CNA**
Quality Review Director
Montebello Rehabilitation Hospital
Baltimore, Maryland

AN ASPEN PUBLICATION®
Aspen Publishers, Inc.
Rockville, Maryland
1989

Library of Congress Cataloging-in-Publication Data

Avillion, Adrianne E.
Quality assurance in rehabilitation nursing: a practical guide/ Adrianne E. Avillion,
Barbara B. Mirgon.
p. cm.
"An Aspen publication."
Includes bibliographies and index.
ISBN: 0-8342-0053-8
1. Rehabilitation nursing–Quality control. I. Mirgon, Barbara B. II. Title
[DNLM: 1. Nursing. 2. Quality Assurance, Health Care.
3. Rehabilitation. WY 150 A958q]
RT120.R4A95 1989 610.73–dc19
DNLM/ DLC
for Library of Congress
88-37144
CIP

Editorial Services: Marsha Davies

Library of Congress Catalog Card Number: 88-37144
ISBN: 0-8342-0053-8

Printed in the United States of America

1 2 3 4 5

# Table of Contents

# Preface

Multiple resources address the operationalization of quality assurance programs in acute care facilities. These resources are inadequate in rehabilitation settings for three major reasons. The first reason, and perhaps the most critical, is the significantly longer length of stay of rehabilitation patients. The average acute care patient spends about a week in the hospital. The average rehabilitation patient, however, spends from 14 days (e.g., for an orthopedic injury) to several months (e.g., after a spinal cord or head injury) within the rehabilitative setting. Length of stay justification depends upon a quality assurance format that addresses the effectiveness of long-term programs.

The second reason is that, in a rehabilitation setting, nursing quality assurance is based on an interdisciplinary team approach in the provision of care. This team concept may be defined as the interaction of health care providers who work together to provide a consistent, goal-oriented approach to rehabilitation. The rehabilitation nursing quality assurance program is greatly influenced by the continual interaction of a multidepartmental system.

Finally, the importance of patient/family involvement in the plan of care is emphasized to a degree seldom seen in acute care. The rehabilitation patient is hospitalized because of an injury and/or illness that alters life style on an often permanent basis. The rehabilitation nurse must help the family unit to reintegrate into a community designed primarily for able-bodied persons. A chronic, disabling condition necessitates long-range planning and extensive postdischarge follow-up. Such necessities mandate a nursing quality assurance program that encompasses consistent, well-documented follow-through on a long-term basis.

Long-term care facilities and community health services experience similar influencing factors. Both are impacted by long-term follow-up considerations and patient/family life style changes. Rehabilitation, long-term care, and community health care have a common focus involving the patient and family—to assist the patient in obtaining maximal potential toward independence. This quality assurance text is designed to address the needs of these settings and to provide guidelines to maximize the quality of long-term programs.

*Adrianne E. Avillion, M.S., R.N., C.R.R.N., C.N.A.*
*Barbara B. Mirgon, B.S.N., R.N., C.N.A.*

# Chapter 1

# Quality Assurance in a Rehabilitation Setting

## INTRODUCTION

Mandating the delivery of high-quality nursing care is not a new concept. The development of standards that measure the effectiveness of nursing practice began as early as 1859, when Florence Nightingale wrote *Notes on Nursing: What It is and What It is Not.*[1] This process of upgrading and evaluating care has reached a pinnacle of importance for today's nurses. At no time in the history of the nursing profession has its quality assurance programs been subjected to such meticulous scrutiny by health care providers and consumers alike.

As health care costs continue to escalate, consumers are demanding increased accountability for both the quality of services provided and justification of expenses. Such demands influence each and every aspect of nursing quality assurance, which, in turn, is influenced by the specific demands of specialty practice. Rehabilitation, one of the fastest-growing specialties in the United States today, is lacking practical information that addresses its quality assurance obligations.

## REHABILITATION AS A HEALTH CARE SPECIALTY

Rehabilitation is the process of restoring persons to their maximal state of wellness. The objectives of rehabilitation nursing reach beyond any inpatient setting; an individual's successful community reintegration depends upon the rehabilitation nurse's knowledge of the societies to which clients must return. Thus, health care professionals who specialize in rehabilitation must provide quality of care in a variety of inpatient and outpatient settings over extended periods of time.

Historically, the problems of handicapped individuals often have been treated in an indifferent fashion, without understanding and without comprehending the degree of adaptation necessary to conduct the activities of daily living. The Bible, which chronicles some of the earliest history of human beings, contains numerous references to the indignities that handicapped people experienced. The blind man, begging for alms outside the Temple, and the lepers, shunned and ridiculed by society, illustrate the public's early negative reaction to disabled individuals.

Because of the many superstitions and the mysticism surrounding religion during the Middle Ages, visibly ill individuals were said to be either cursed or possessed by the Devil. This belief in demons persisted well into the 18th century. In the 19th century, the growth and economic importance of industries sparked the passage of national health policies that concentrated on the industrial worker. Legislation was passed making industrial establishments responsible for injuries to employees. However, there were no real efforts to assist the disabled to function successfully in society until the 20th century.

The polio epidemics of the 1930s and 1940s stirred interest in rehabilitation when countless persons were left paralyzed by the devastating disease. This interest escalated following World War II, when thousands of disabled GIs returned home. One of the earliest rehabilitation pioneers was Dr. Howard Rusk, who conceived his philosophy and concept of physical medicine and rehabilitation while directing the Army Air Corps Convalescent and Rehabilitation Services during World War II. In 1946, Dr. Rusk continued his rehabilitation work as a civilian at Bellevue Hospital in New York City. He found that his struggles to rehabilitate his patients were sometimes hampered by the negative attitudes of health care personnel, and progress was painfully slow.[2]

Steps were gradually taken toward normalizing society's acceptance of the disabled. In December 1955, the World Rehabilitation Fund was founded. Its purpose was to sponsor international projects that would help the handicapped and create a better understanding of them and their problems. As the organization grew, additional objectives were identified. Health professionals were trained in the rehabilitation field, and efforts to increase employment opportunities for the handicapped were expanded.[3]

In 1973 the Rehabilitation Act made a significant impact on issues concerning the handicapped. Section 501 required the development of affirmative action programs for employment of handicapped individuals in departments of the executive branch of the federal government. Discrimination against applicants and employees of the federal government solely on grounds of disability was forbidden.[4]

Section 502 established the Architectural and Transportation Barriers Compliance Board to develop standards for compliance with regulations to overcome architectural, transportation, and communication barriers in public facilities and residential/institutional housing.[5] The affirmative action plan (Section 503) required that contractors receiving $2500 or more from the federal government must recruit, hire, and advance qualified disabled individuals. Section 504 set standards for nondiscrimination in hiring under federal contracts and stated that disabled children and youth are entitled to a free, appropriate public education in a setting as close to normal as possible.[6]

A set of standards for making buildings and facilities accessible to and usable by physically handicapped people was published by the American National Standards Institute in 1983. Its specifications are recommended for adoption and enforcement by administrative authorities in the construction and alteration of buildings and site development so that optimal accessibility is achieved.[7]

Today, rehabilitation is a highly respected, rapidly growing specialty. According to the National Association of Rehabilitation Facilities, as of June 1987 there were 83 free-standing rehabilitation hospitals and 524 rehabilitation units within acute care facilities devoted to the practice of physical medicine and rehabilitation. These figures indicate an approximate increase of 30 percent within the last three years.[8] If this trend continues, there will be a 100 percent increase in the number of rehabilitation beds in this country by the year 2000. What are the reasons for such a tremendous expansion of rehabilitation services? The answer is threefold: the prospective payment system, consumer needs, and the rising cost of health care services.

## PROSPECTIVE PAYMENT SYSTEM

In 1983, Congress directed that Medicare develop a prospective payment system based on diagnosis-related groups (DRGs) for acute hospital care. The prospective payment system pays the acute hospital a fixed payment for each Medicare admission. The level of payment varies depending on which of the 492 DRGs describes the patient's condition. Presently, rehabilitation hospitals and rehabilitation units within acute care hospitals are exempt from the prospective payment system. This exemption arose from concern that the acute care DRG patient classification system and its payment approach would be inappropriate for inpatient rehabilitative care.[9]

Rehabilitation emphasizes the treatment of functional limitations and promotes maximal independent functioning. Such treatment usually follows a period of acute medical and/or surgical services and often precedes some form of home health, outpatient, or nursing home care. It may be probable that functional status, rather than a diagnostic grouping, determines the length and cost of rehabilitation stays.[10] Regardless of the reasons for DRG exemption, the fact remains that rehabilitation facilities are temporarily free from the time constraints placed on acute facilities by a prospective payment system that provides Medicare reimbursement only for the number of days allotted by a particular diagnostic group.

Thus, acute care is under considerable pressure to complete treatment within a rigidly defined period of time. Rehabilitation facilities, therefore, must be prepared to deal with "quicker and sicker" admissions. Patients who, prior to DRGs, may have begun rehabilitation within acute care are now being transferred rapidly. Rehabilitation hospitals and units must have beds to accept patients more quickly and the staff to care for them. Rehabilitation nurses are promoting wellness restoration while dealing with the admission of patients who may be more acutely ill and less medically stable. Such trends are influencing not only present rehabilitation needs but are having a critical impact on the specialty's future quality assurance needs.

## CONSUMER NEEDS

There is a critical need for rehabilitation services in this country. The number of Americans with physical disabilities is increasing at a significant rate.[11] Thanks to continuing advances in medical technology, persons are surviving once-fatal occurrences of traumatic injuries or illnesses. As the population grows, so does the number of disabled citizens. The disabled population can be roughly profiled according to age.

The first age group is infancy. Infants born with serious birth defects are surviving in record numbers. Persons with birth injuries (due to premature births or congenital defects) may require rehabilitation services for many years, throughout various stages of growth and development, even throughout life.[12] In order to live productive, satisfying lives, these children must be provided with adequate rehabilitation services.

A second group of patients are those who have experienced traumatic injury from accidents, resulting in brain and spinal cord injury. These persons are usually young adults who comprise a significant portion of the work force. If rehabilitation services were not available for this group, the economic impact on society would be devastating. The drain on public welfare systems would be enormous. However, it has been estimated that by maximizing patients' capabilities, "rehabilitation's pay-off in actual work, tax dollars, and return on the cost of rehabilitation services has been estimated at between eight and ten dollars for each dollar spent."[13] The best true indicator, however, of the effectiveness of rehabilitation is the quality of life for disabled citizens.

The majority of patients requiring rehabilitation services are those who are disabled as a result of chronic illnesses. These persons are typically middle-aged or older. This elderly population is the fastest-growing age group in the United States. It is also the age group in which chronic illness is most prevalent. As the number of senior citizens increases, rehabilitation needs must be assessed in terms of the geriatric population.

Currently, one of every four Americans between 55 and 64 years of age is seriously disabled. More than 11 percent of the people in the United States are over 65. By the year 2030, 55 million Americans, or nearly one person in five, will be over the age of 65. Health care providers will soon be spending about half of their time caring for the elderly. Currently, nearly 30 percent of all health care dollars are spent on persons 65 and older.[14]

In summary, as a result of advances in health care technology, the physically disabled are living longer and requiring continuing care. It is estimated that in less than a decade rehabilitation facilities and personnel will be totally inadequate to meet the country's needs.[15] Thus, rehabilitation services must be provided for a population increasing both in numbers and in age and who are experiencing skyrocketing health care costs as well.

## IMPACT OF COST

From 1985 to 1986, health care spending increased by 8.4 percent.[16] Those persons responsible for the disbursement of insurance dollars are monitoring the allocation of those dollars in terms of costs and the patient's documented progress in a planned rehabilitation program. It is not unreasonable to expect the patient to receive the needed care in a cost-efficient manner and in the appropriate setting. Now more than ever, consumers (identified as insurance payers and the general public) have a vested interest in the cost and quality of care.

Rehabilitation is a highly complex form of care requiring longer lengths of stay than acute care. The average length of stay in acute care is estimated at 6.5 days.[17] In rehabilitation, lengths of stay can range from about two weeks for an orthopedic injury to several months for a patient who has suffered a head injury. As previously noted, decreasing lengths of stay for acute care are causing the admission of "quicker and sicker" rehabilitation patients.

Rehabilitation constitutes less than 3 percent of all health services, but payments are two to three times higher than acute care payments in comparable DRGs. More than half of rehabilitation's revenue comes from services to Medicare beneficiaries with chronic diseases.[18] The lack of universal definitions of functional status measures and patient outcomes in rehabilitation further aggravates efforts to mitigate costs.

Competition among rehabilitation facilities for qualified personnel also contributes to spiraling health care costs. The current shortages of skilled personnel, particularly rehabilitation nurses, have forced hospitals to offer a variety of recruitment inducements. One such inducement is a higher benefit and salary package, which, in turn, adds to increasing hospital costs. However, the most attractive recruitment options cannot attract staff if the staff members themselves simply do not exist. Many rehabilitation providers agree that lack of training and orientation to the specialty is a major cause of inadequate care for the disabled population.[19] Public demand for cost containment will accelerate competition among rehabilitation facilities to provide quality care with positive patient outcomes in the shortest possible period of time.

## REHABILITATION QUALITY ASSURANCE

Quality assurance is the objective and systematic assessment, planning, implementation, and evaluation of the quality and appropriateness of patient care. This includes identifying measures that improve care and resolve problems or potential problems. Quality assurance is the measure by which to develop a health care-conscious and cost-conscious program needed for future health care services.

Rehabilitation quality assurance differs from acute care quality assurance in several facets of its scope of practice. Rehabilitation facilities are experiencing unprecedented growth as well as significantly longer lengths of stay as compared with acute care facilities. The justification for such longer lengths of stay depends upon a quality assurance format that addresses the effectiveness of long-term programs.

Emphasis on the interdisciplinary team is another major difference between acute care and rehabilitation nursing quality assurance. Departmental quality assurance plans are only a part of the picture. Each team (e.g., brain injury, stroke, or spinal cord injury) is involved in the assessment, planning, implementation, and evaluation of its programs, thus ensuring that the patient and family receive the most beneficial program and achieve maximal functioning capacity. As stated in the rehabilitation nursing Standard VII, "the nurse collaborates with the interdisciplinary team in assessing, planning, implementing, and evaluating the individual's care, rehabilitation program, and related rehabilitation activities."[20] What factors does the team use in this interdisciplinary program evaluation effort?

It must be remembered that the goal of rehabilitation is to restore maximal functioning. One measure of success is the extent to which patients are able to return to their respective communities, although this may be influenced by the availability of community supportive services and the patient's own family support system.[21] More direct measures of program effectiveness may include mobility status and the ability of the patient to perform activities of daily living.

Mobility status may be measured by comparing independent mobility without versus with assisting devices (e.g., cane, wheelchair, walker, and the like) and whether the patient needs the assistance of another person to be safely mobile. The ability to perform activities of daily living may be classified according to the amount and type of assistance needed and the ability to perform tasks safely and accurately. Additional considerations include the effect of medical complications during rehabilitation, the coexistence of other medical conditions, the length of time from onset of trauma and/or illness, and the initiation of comprehensive rehabilitation services.

All factors must be measured against similar rehabilitation categories. For example, reliable measurements would not be obtained if the functional outcomes of a 22-year-old paraplegic were compared with those of a 65-year-old stroke patient. Likewise, the comparison of 18-year-old and 70-year-old patients with head injuries must consider the variables present in such a widely differing age span. Program evaluations must consider and allow for the impacting variables of age, pre-injury/illness health status, motivation, and family support, to name a few.

Nurses, as an integral component of the rehabilitation team, must function not only as team members participating in overall program evaluation, but also within the traditional role of the nursing profession. As further stated in the *Standards of Rehabilitation Nursing Practice*, "The nurse participates in peer review and interdisciplinary program evaluation to assure that high quality nursing care is provided to individuals in a rehabilitation setting."[22] The rationale for this standard states:

> Evaluation of the quality of nursing care through examination of the nursing process and the outcomes related to nursing diagnosis is one way to fulfill the profession's obligation to ensure adherence to professional practice standards. Peer review, interdisciplinary program evaluation, risk management, and nursing quality assurance studies are used in the endeavor.[23]

Additionally, the rehabilitation nurse must help the family unit to reintegrate into a society designed primarily for able-bodied persons. A chronic, disabling condition necessitates long-range planning and lengthy follow up. Such necessities mandate a nursing quality assurance program that encompasses consistent, well-documented follow-through on a long-term basis.

Rehabilitation quality assurance will also contribute to the development of a prospective payment system for the specialty. Data collected via quality assurance mechanisms will provide implications for such a system as well as criteria for its success. Meaningful and reliable measures of functional status may form the basis of a rehabilitation prospective payment system. Designing an outcome-based system would also promote a cost-effective method of delivering quality care and possibly provide predictions of average lengths of rehabilitative stay.

A very important component of any rehabilitation prospective payment system must also consider the critical need for patient education. The time constraints placed on acute care services mandate that the majority of patient educational needs be provided in the rehabilitation sector. How does patient education impact on functional status? Do successful rehabilitation outcomes depend on this education and, if so, to what extent? These factors must be considered as a rehabilitation prospective payment system is developed. Quality assurance programs must monitor the impact of patient education on rehabilitation outcomes so that adequate teaching time is included in any proposed prospective payment system.

## OTHER REGULATORY SYSTEMS

### Tax Equity and Fiscal Responsibility Act

In addition to prospective payment systems there are several other systems that may impact on quality assurance programs. The actual mandate to develop prospective reimbursement for health care was issued in 1982 when the Tax Equity and Fiscal Responsibility Act (TEFRA) was enacted. TEFRA's major hospital reimbursement changes were

- a limit on total inpatient costs per discharge, adjusted to reflect each hospital's case mix (the numbers and types of patients treated in a hospital)
- a limit on the annual rate of increase of total costs per discharge
- a small incentive payment for hospitals that keep costs below both of these limits [24]

These interim reforms were accompanied by a provision that directed the secretary of Health and Human Services to propose long-range Medicare reimbursement reforms. Thus, the current prospective payment system based on DRGs came into being.

Under a prospective payment system, physician involvement in the hospital administrative team is imperative if the financial responsibilities of the hospital are to be met. In a rehabilitation facility, where prospective payment is still in the planning stages, physicians should be part of the health care team researching concepts such as functional status measures. Currently, physicians are already deeply involved in reviewing quality of care issues under the existing prospective payment system as shown in the role of peer review organizations.

### Peer Review Organizations

Peer review organizations are federally funded physician organizations under contract to the Department of Health and Human Services. These organizations review quality of care and determine whether payment should be made for hospital care provided under the Medicare program. Determinations are made by reviewing a percentage of about one-third of all services provided to Medicare beneficiaries to establish whether care was reasonable, was medically necessary, and met professionally recognized quality standards.[25]

What impact will peer review organizations have on the practice of rehabilitation? Generic standards of measurement must be established so that an accurate prospective payment system can be formulated and appropriately reviewed by peer review organizations.

## Preferred Provider Organization

A preferred provider organization is a payment arrangement whereby consumers contract with hospitals or physicians on a negotiated fee-for-service basis to provide health care services.[26] Consumers are given financial incentives (usually reduced or eliminated copayments or deductibles) to use providers associated with preferred provider organizations. Incentives may also include coverage of a broader range of services or simplified claims processing.[27]

Preferred provider organizations are not standardized. Thus, the provision of quality care lacks generic measurements with which to evaluate provided services. The rapid growth of rehabilitation services makes the specialty a likely target for the development of future preferred provider organizations founded on rehabilitation needs.

## Health Care Financing Administration

The Health Care Financing Administration is the component of the United States Department of Health and Human Services that administers the Medicare and Medicaid programs. As part of its quality assurance endeavors, the Health Care Financing Administration reviews and screens the following data.

- adequacy of discharge planning
- medical stability of the patient at discharge
- deaths
- nosocomial infections
- unscheduled return to surgery within the same admission for the same condition
- trauma suffered in the hospital[28]

Screening criteria for quality review have thus been established by federal government organizations. Such measures most likely will influence any attempt to define measures of rehabilitation functional status. Any person establishing a rehabilitation quality assurance program should be familiar with government organizations and their screening criteria. These criteria will certainly set precedents for any regulatory systems to be devised for rehabilitation.

## SUMMARY

Rehabilitation is the process of restoring a person to the maximal state of wellness. Health care professionals specializing in rehabilitation must provide quality of care in a variety of settings over extended periods of time.

Historically, the problems of disabled individuals have often been treated in an indifferent fashion. It was not until the 20th century that real efforts were made to assist the disabled to function successfully in society. Today, however, rehabilitation is one of the most rapidly growing specialties in the country.

There are several reasons for the increased need for rehabilitation services. Acute care hospitals are under considerable pressure to complete treatment within a period of time defined by the current prospective payment system. Rehabilitation facilities (and rehabilitation units within acute care hospitals) are presently exempt from this system and must be able to accept patients who are being transferred from acute care more quickly than ever before. These patients may also be more acutely ill and less medically stable.

Thanks to continuing advances in medical technology, persons are surviving once-fatal occurrences of birth defects, traumatic injuries, or chronic illnesses. The majority of patients requiring rehabilitative services are those who are disabled as a result of chronic illness. The age group in which chronic illness is most prevalent is the elderly population. This is also the fastest-growing age group in the United States. Thus, rehabilitation services must be provided for a population increasing both in numbers and in age.

Finally, the impact of cost is significant. Insurance dollars will be allotted in terms of documented progress in a cost-efficient, successful, planned rehabilitation program.

Rehabilitation quality assurance differs from acute care quality assurance in several ways. The rehabilitation field is experiencing unprecedented growth as well as significantly longer lengths of stay as compared with acute care facilities. Emphasis on the interdisciplinary team and the need to develop reliable measures of functional status for program evaluation are also critical differences. Finally, the specialty is in the process of gathering data to recommend its own prospective payment system. Public demand for cost containment will increase competition among rehabilitation facilities to provide quality care with positive patient outcomes in the shortest possible period of time.

## NOTES

1. Florence Nightingale, *Notes on Nursing: What It Is and What It Is Not* (New York: Dover Publications, 1969), xviii.

2. Howard A. Rusk, *A World To Care For* (New York: Random House, Inc., 1972), 1–140.

3. Ibid.

4. Christina M. Mumma, ed., *Rehabilitation Nursing: Concepts and Practice—A Core Curriculum*, 2nd ed. (Evanston, Ill.: Rehabilitation Nursing Foundation, 1987), 8.

5. Ibid.

6. Ibid.

7. American National Standards, *Specifications for Making Buildings and Facilities Accessible to and Usable by Physically Handicapped People* (New York: American National Standards Institute, 1983).

8. National Association of Rehabilitation Facilities Headquarters, telephone interview, June 1987.

9. Susan Hosek et al., *Charges and Outcomes for Rehabilitative Care—Implications for the Prospective Payment System* (Santa Monica, Calif.: Rand Corporation, 1986), v.

10. Ibid.

11. Brent England, Cathy Amkraut, and Michael Lespane, "An Agenda for Medical Rehabilitation—1987 and into the 21st Century," a paper—Section for Rehabilitation Hospitals and Programs, American Hospital Association; Washington Business Group on Health, Institute for Rehabilitation and Disability Management, Washington, D.C., 1987, 2.

12. Ibid., 4–5.

13. Ibid., 6.

14. U.S. Department of Health and Human Services, National Institutes of Health, National Institute on Aging, *Progress Report on Geriatric Medicine*, NIH Publication #82-2307, September 1982, prepared by Ann Dieffenbach for the White House Conference on Aging, 4.

15. England, Amkraut, and Lespane, "An Agenda for Medical Rehabilitation," 2.

16. "Government Releases 1986 Health Care Spending Data," in *American College of Utilization Review Physicians Newsletter*, ed. James T. Menges, 14, no. 7 (August 1987): 6.

17. "AIDS Hospital Admissions Rise," in *American College of Utilization Review Physicians Newsletter*, ed. James T. Menges, 14, no. 7 (August 1987): 7.

18. England, Amkraut, and Lespane, "An Agenda for Medical Rehabilitation," 8–12.

19. Ibid., 9.

20. American Nurses' Association and Association of Rehabilitation Nurses, *Standards of Rehabilitation Nursing Practice* (Kansas City, Mo.: American Nurses' Association, 1986), 10.

21. Hosek et al., *Charges and Outcomes for Rehabilitative Care*, 34.

22. American Nurses' Association and Association of Rehabilitation Nurses, *Standards of Rehabilitation Nursing Practice*, 11.

23. Ibid.

24. Howard Smith and Myron D. Fottler, *Prospective Payment* (Rockville, Md.: Aspen Publishers, Inc., 1985), 15.

25. American Hospital Association, *Communicating Quality Care* (Chicago: American Hospital Association, 1987), 6, 25.

26. Ibid., 6.

27. H. Griffith, "Who Will Become the Preferred Providers?" *American Journal of Nursing* 85

(1985): 539.

28. American Hospital Association, *Communicating Quality Care*, 26.

---

## BIBLIOGRAPHY

American National Standards. *Specifications for Making Buildings and Facilities Accessible to and Usable by Physically Handicapped People.* New York: American National Standards Institute, 1983.

Amkraut, C. "Washington File: Disability Payment Reforms in Public Private Sectors on Return to Work." *Business and Health,* March 1987.

Commission for Administrative Services in Hospitals. *A Quality Control Plan for Nursing Service.* Los Angeles: Commission for Administrative Services in Hospitals, 1965.

Coopers & Lybrand, National Association of Rehabilitation Facilities (NARF). *NARF Position Paper on the Prospective Payment System,* 1986.

Dock, Lavinia L. *A Short History of Nursing.* New York: G.P. Putman's Sons, 1925.

Galvin, D.E. "Health Promotion, Disability Management, and Rehabilitation in the Workplace." *Rehabilitation Literature* 47 (1971): 9–10.

Graham, Nancy O., ed. *Quality Assurance in Hospitals.* Rockville, Md.: Aspen Publishers, Inc., 1982.

Hamilton, B., principal investigator, 716/845-2201, State University of New York at Buffalo (SUNY). A database documenting severity of patient disability and the outcomes of medical rehabilitation. *Uniform National Data System Update,* 1987.

Harman, Carol A. "Involving Staff in Nursing Quality Assurance." *Quality Review Bulletin* 6 (1980): 26-30.

Hirshberg, C.G.; Lewis, L.; and Vaughn, P. *Rehabilitation: A Manual for the Care of the Disabled and Elderly.* Philadelphia: J.B. Lippincott Co., 1976.

Meisenheimer, Claire Gavin. "Quality Assurance: Its Origins, Transformations, and Projects." In *Quality Assurance,* edited by Claire Gavin Meisenheimer. Rockville, Md.: Aspen Publishers, Inc., 1985.

Moore, Karen R. "Nurses Learn from Nursing Audit." *Nursing Outlook* 27 (1979): 254–258.

Moore, Karen R. "Quality Assurance and Nursing Audit: Are They Effective?" *Nursing Management* 13 (1982): 18–22.

Nightingale, Florence. *Notes on Matters Affecting the Health, Efficiency, and Hospital Administration of the British Army.* St. Mark's Lane, W.C.: Harrison and Sons, 1858.

Nightingale, Florence. *Notes on Nursing: What It Is and What It Is Not.* New York: Dover Publications, 1969.

Padilla, Geraldine V., and Grant, Marcia M. "Quality Assurance Programs for Nursing." *Journal of Advanced Nursing* 7 (1982): 135-145.

Phaneuf, Maria C. *The Nursing Audit and Self-Regulation in Nursing Practice.* New York: Appleton-Century-Crofts, 1976.

Phaneuf, Maria C., and Wandelt, Mabel A. "Obstacles to and Potentials for Nursing Quality Appraisal." *Quality Review Bulletin* 7 (1981): 2–5.

Rehabilitation International. A report of legislative, government policy, advocacy, legal affairs, and technical matters concerning disabled persons that were discussed at a national conference on legislation in Vienna, Austria. *Report from International Rehabilitation Conference on Legislation,* 1987.

Rosen, E., and Fox, I.G. *Abnormal Psychology*. Philadelphia: W.B. Saunders Co., 1972.

Russel, H. *Affirmative Action for Disabled People*. Washington, D.C.: U.S. Government Printing Office, 1973.

Salfilios-Rothschild, C. *The Sociology and Social Psychology of Disability and Rehabilitation*. New York: Random House, Inc., 1970.

*The Way: The Living Bible, Catholic Edition*. Wheaton, Ill.: Tyndale House, 1976.

Weinstein, Edwin L. "Developing a Measure of the Quality of Nursing Care." *Journal of Nursing Administration* 6, no. 1 (1976): 1–3

Whitten, E.B. "The Rehabilitation Act of 1973 and the Severely Disabled." *Journal of Rehabilitation* (July–August 1974): 39–40.

Yura, Helen, and Walsh, Mary B. *The Nursing Process*. Washington, D.C.: Catholic University of America Press, 1967.

Zimmer, Marie J., guest ed. "Quality Assurance." *Nursing Clinics of North America* 9 (1974).

---

## SUGGESTED READINGS

Acton, N. "The World's Response to Disability: Evolution of a Philosophy." *Archives of Physical Medicine and Rehabilitation* 63 (1982): 145–149.

American Hospital Association. *Communicating Quality Care*. Chicago: American Hospital Association, 1987.

American Nurses' Association. *Nursing: A Social Policy Statement*. Kansas City, Mo.: American Nurses' Association, 1980.

Andrews, Melvin J. "TEFRA, DRG's, PPS, Etc." In *A Study Guide in Quality Assurance and Utilization Review*. Produced by the American College of Utilization Review Physicians, edition of June 1986.

Carpenter-Mason, Beverly. "Understanding TEFRA, PPS, and DRG's—A Q/A Perspective." In *A Study Guide in Quality Assurance and Utilization Review*. Produced by the American College of Utilization Review Physicians, edition of June 1986.

Carter, Joan H., and Hilliard, Mildred. *Standards of Nursing Care*. New York: Springer, 1972.

Del Polito, Gene A. "Prospective Payment: A Sign of Changing Times." *Journal of Medical Technology* 1 (1984): 1.

Eckenhoff, E.A. "The Value of the Disabled Life." In *Comprehensive Rehabilitation Nursing*, edited by N. Martin, N.B. Holt, and D. Hicks. New York: McGraw-Hill Book Co., 1981.

Falcone, A.R. "Capitalizing on Prospective Reimbursement with a New Utilization System." *Quality Review Bulletin* 10 (1984): 316–324.

Fifer, W.R., "Beyond Peer Review: The Medical Staff Role in the Price-Competitive System." *Quality Review Bulletin* 10 (1984): 262–268.

Flanagan, Lyndia. *One Strong Voice*. Kansas City, Mo.: American Nurses' Association, 1976.

Franz, J. "Challenge for Nursing: Hiking Productivity without Lowering Quality of Care." *Modern Healthcare* no. 12 (1984), 60–64, 68.

Froebe, Doris J., and Bain, R. Joyce. *Quality Assurance Programs and Controls in Nursing*. St. Louis, Mo.: C.V. Mosby Co., 1976.

Graham, Nancy O., ed. *Quality Assurance in Hospitals*. Rockville, Md.: Aspen Publishers, Inc., 1982.

Hamburg, D.A., and Adams, J.E. "A Perspective on Coping Behavior." *Archives of General Psychiatry* 17 (1967): 142–153.

Jeffrey, D.A. "A Living Environment for the Physically Disabled." *Rehabilitation Literature* 49 (1973): 757–762.

Lang, Norma M. "Quality Assurance in Nursing." *AORN Journal* 22 (1975): 180–186.

Lipp, C.S. "The Effect of the Prospective Payment System on Hospital QA/UR Systems. *Quality Review Bulletin* 10 (1984): 283–287.

Marriner, Ann. "The Research Process in Quality Assurance." *American Journal of Nursing* 79 (1979): 2158–2161.

Maslow, A.H. *Motivation and Personality.* New York: Harper & Row, 1970.

Miller, M. Clinton III, and Knapp, Rebecca Grant. *Evaluating Quality of Care.* Rockville, Md.: Aspen Publishers, Inc., 1979.

Nightingale, Florence. *Notes on Nursing: What It Is and What It Is Not.* New York: Dover Publications, 1969.

Phaneuf, Maria C., and Wandelt, Mabel A. "Quality Assurance in Nursing." *Nursing Forum* 13 (1974): 328–345.

Phaneuf, Maria C., and Wandelt, Mabel A. "Obstacles to and Potentials for Nursing Quality Appraisal." *Quality Review Bulletin* 7 (1981): 2–5.

Prescott, Patricia. "Evaluation Research: Issues in Evaluation of Nursing Programs." *Nursing Administration Quarterly* 2 (1978): 63–80.

Rusk, Howard A. *A World To Care For.* New York: Random House, Inc., 1972.

Russel, H. *Affirmative Action for Disabled People.* Washington, D.C.: U.S. Government Printing Office, 1973.

Schlotfedt, Rosella M. "Problems in the Development of Adequate Criteria." *Nursing Research* 11 (1962): 208–211.

Schmied, Elsie, "Living with Cost Containment." *Journal of Nursing Administration* 10 (1980): 1147.

Stevens, Barbara. "Analysis of Trends in Nursing Care Management." *Journal of Nursing Administration* 2, no. 6 (1972): 12–17.

Tobias, Richard B. "The DRG Picture." In *A Study Guide in Quality Assurance and Utilization Review.* Produced by the American College of Utilization Review Physicians, edition of June 1986.

Ventura, Marlene R. "Correlation between the Quality Patient Care Scale and Phaneuf Audit." *International Journal of Nursing Studies* 17 (1980): 155-162.

Watson, Annita, and Mayers, Marlene. "Evaluating the Quality of Patient Care through Retrospective Chart Review." *Journal of Nursing Administration* 6, no. 2 (1976): 17–21.

Weinstein, Edwin, L. "Developing a Measure of the Quality of Nursing Care." *Journal of Nursing Administration* 6, no. 1 (1976): 1–3.

Zimmer, Marie J. "A Model for Evaluating Nursing Care." *Hospitals* 48 (1974): 91–95, 131.

Zimmer, Marie J., guest ed. "Quality Assurance." *Nursing Clinics of North America* 9 (1974).

# Chapter 2

# Integrating Standards in a Rehabilitation Nursing Quality Assurance Program

## INTRODUCTION

According to Webster, a standard is "something that is established by authority, custom, or general consent as a model or example to be followed."[1] The nursing profession is governed by many such standards. Some of these are strict internal regulatory measures such as state nurse practice acts. Others, such as the standards of the Commission on the Accreditation of Rehabilitation Facilities, are followed voluntarily in order to assure consumers of a specific degree of excellence in specialty services. Regardless of motivation, standards shape the process of evaluating nursing care. The nursing quality assurance committee must familiarize itself with the norms that guide nursing practice. Specialty hospitals, such as rehabilitation facilities, must also adhere to practice standards that monitor specialty practices. The nursing departments of such hospitals will need quality assurance programs that monitor the aspects of rehabilitation nursing in accordance with all relevant standards.

## JOINT COMMISSION ON ACCREDITATION OF HEALTHCARE ORGANIZATIONS

### Historical Background

In 1918, the American College of Surgeons established the Hospital Standardization Program, which encouraged the adoption of a uniform medical record format to record accurately a patient's clinical course.[2] Over the years the program gradually expanded its content to define the optimal setting in which inpatient health care services should be provided. As hospitals became increasingly sophisticated and complex, the program's standards needed frequent updating to keep abreast of contemporary health care. By 1951, the program had become a serious financial burden to the College of Surgeons. Therefore, the American College of Surgeons, the American College of Physicians, the American Hospital Association, the American Medical Association, and the Canadian Medical Association founded the Joint Commission on Accreditation of Hospitals—renamed the Joint Commission on Accreditation of Healthcare Organizations (Joint Commission) in 1987. The new organization's purpose was to encourage voluntary attainment of uniformly high standards of institutional medical care.[3]

The standards developed by the American College of Surgeons were adopted by the Joint Commission. On January 1, 1952, the Joint Commission officially began to review hospitals and grant accreditation. In 1965, Medicare was enacted. A provision of the Medicare Act was that participating hospitals must be Joint Commission-accredited. *Without accreditation, a hospital is ineligible for government funds.*

The Medicare Act demonstrated government confidence in the Joint Commission. This confidence stimulated the board of commissioners to reevaluate their standards to attain two objectives.

1. to raise and strengthen the standards from their present level of minimum essential to the level of optimal achievable and to assure their suitability to the modern state of the art
2. to simplify and clarify the language of standards and interpretations to remove all possible ambiguities and misunderstandings[4]

The Joint Commission has continued to update and reevaluate its standards, revising its accreditation manuals annually. The organization's purpose, however, has remained the same: to "encourage the voluntary attainment of uniformly high standards of institutional medical care."[5]

In 1974, the Joint Commission added quality assurance to its standards. In 1979, new quality assurance standards were introduced, and nursing departments were required to examine nursing care via ongoing programs that develop and implement plans for correction and evaluation of nursing care. These quality assurance standards were again revised in 1984 to include documentation of findings, corrective actions taken, and an annual reappraisal of a hospital's quality assurance program.[6]

In December 1987, the Joint Commission described a multifaceted approach for change that included five major components.

1. *Selection of clinical indicators.* Clinical performance indicators that describe the most valid clinical outcomes need to be identified.
2. *Development of case mix adjustment capability.* In order to use the clinical

indicator data effectively, adjustments need to be made for case mix differences.

3. *Identification of key organizational characteristics.* The Joint Commission is now focusing on identifying the organizational and management factors that characterize the "excellent health care organization."

4. *Improvement in the monitoring between surveys.* The intent of this component is to develop an ongoing and interactive system between the Joint Commission and hospitals. Each indicator will be monitored and used to evaluate performance against standards.

5. *Improvement in the survey process.* By 1992, the Joint Commission intends to develop a new conceptual framework for a new survey process.[7]

As evidenced by the five components for change, quality assurance continues to grow in both scope and importance. At the November 18, 1987, meeting of the Maryland Hospital Association's Quality Leadership Assembly, the president of the Joint Commission focused his remarks on these components of change. Dennis O'Leary, M.D., noted that there is a shift in quality assessment priorities toward defining and gathering information that directly affects the quality of patient care. Priorities should be adjusted so that incentives are created for the hospitals to find problems and solve them. These priorities will become even more important as the public's demand for health care organizations to be accountable for the quality of care they provide increases.[8]

Assuring the consumer of a specific degree of excellence is the responsibility of all health care providers. However, the chairperson of the nursing quality assurance committee bears the additional burden of functioning as the "expert" as well as the primary resource person for the nursing department's program of quality assurance. How can she or he prepare for this critical task? One approach would be to formulate a logical method of reviewing essential standards and their various components. The chairperson should be able to answer the following questions satisfactorily.

## Joint Commission Standard Compliance

*Does the Nursing Quality Assurance Chairperson Have the Latest Joint Commission Accreditation Manual?* Although the answer may seem to be self-evident, it is disconcerting to realize that many institutions rely on outdated copies with which to prepare for an accreditation visit. The nursing quality assurance chairperson should possess the most recent available accreditation data, including not only the sections on nursing quality assurance but the sections on the hospital quality assurance program, the standards for the entire nursing department, and any specific sections relating to specialty areas. Remember, quality assurance affects every facet of the nursing department, which, in turn, powerfully impacts on the hospital quality assurance program as a whole. An extensive physical rehabilitation services section is included in the 1988 manual. The nursing quality assurance chairperson should have quick and easy access to all of these sections of the Joint Commission manual.

*Is the Interrelationship between the Hospital Quality Assurance Committee and the Nursing Quality Assurance Committee Effectively Demonstrated?* The chairperson of the nursing quality assurance committee should hold regular membership on the hospital quality assurance committee. (The role of the chairperson is described in detail in Chapter 3.) In this way, a system of regular communication is established among all departments and correlated by the facility's quality assurance director. Interdisciplinary projects can be developed, initiated, and evaluated by the committee and documented in the meeting minutes.

The basic purpose of quality assurance is the same, whether it is on a hospitalwide or departmental level. The first Joint Commission standard governing hospital quality assurance is:

> There is an ongoing quality assurance program designed to objectively and systematically monitor and evaluate the quality and appropriateness of patient care, pursue opportunities to improve patient care, and resolve identified problems.[9]

Similarly, the nursing department's quality assurance mandate states that:

> As part of the hospital's quality assurance program, the quality and appropriateness of the patient care provided by the nursing department/ service are monitored and evaluated, and identified problems are resolved.[10]

The ultimate aim, therefore, is the continual delivery of high-quality care within a system that not only monitors and evaluates services but that solves problems of service delivery.

*Does the Nursing Quality Assurance Program Satisfy the Standard's Required Characteristics?* A standard's required characteristics describe the means by which to achieve the standard. In the instance of nursing quality assurance, all major clinical functions of the department must be monitored and evaluated by

- routinely collecting information about important aspects of nursing care
- assessing collected data to identify problems and methods of improving care
- identifying objective evaluation criteria that reflect current knowledge and clinical experience
- ensuring that when patient care problems or opportunities to improve care are identified actions are taken and their effectiveness is evaluated
- documenting the findings and conclusions of monitoring, evaluation, and problem-solving activities
- documenting actions taken to resolve problems and improve patient care
- annually reappraising the nursing department's quality assurance program[11]

The nursing quality assurance program must reflect all of the required characteristics so that the appropriate Joint Commission standards are achieved.

*Does the Nursing Quality Assurance Program Reflect the Required Characteristics of the Joint Commission Standards for Physical Rehabilitation?* In the 1988 Joint Commission manual, the chapter devoted to physical rehabilitation services "describes the nature of services in programs or units that promote the restoration of the functional abilities of individuals with physical, cognitive, and/or sensoriperceptual impairment."[12]

It is important to familiarize oneself with the entire chapter. The following standards and required characteristics, however, seem to identify the most critical concepts for the nursing quality assurance committee's attention.

As part of the hospital's quality assurance program, the quality and appropriateness of patient care provided by any physical rehabilitation service, whether provided singly, in combination, or as part of a comprehensive physical rehabilitation program or unit, are monitored and evaluated, and identified problems are resolved.[13]

This particular standard is nearly identical to the hospital and nursing quality assurance initial standards. Thus, if the quality assurance program satisfies one of these standards, it should satisfy all three of them.

As would be expected, the emphasis is on interdisciplinary involvement and promotion of optimal functional status. These factors highlight the major differences between the Joint Commission's standards for acute care and rehabilitation.

- Rehabilitation nursing services are designed to provide for the prevention of complications of physical disability, the restoration of optimal functioning, and adaptation to an altered life style through the use of the nursing process...

- As appropriate, rehabilitation nurses collaborate with the patient, the family, and other health care providers and agencies in regard to discharge planning and teaching.

- Rehabilitation nursing services staff monitors the degree to which the individualized nursing care goals for each patient are achieved.[14]

The nursing quality assurance program must demonstrate compliance in these areas. Such compliance may be more difficult to document for a rehabilitation unit within an acute care facility. Methods for nursing quality assurance in both free-standing rehabilitation facilities and units within acute care are discussed thoroughly in later chapters. Regardless of location, these standards must be met and compliance documented.

*Does the Chairperson Have Access to the Latest Joint Commission Publications, Newsletters, Bulletins, and Continuing Education Announcements?* The nursing quality assurance chairperson may not directly receive this information. Who does? It may be the hospital's chief executive officer, the director of nursing, or staff development personnel. The chairperson must know who receives mailings and arrange to have easy access to the information. Again, the importance of keeping up to date cannot be overemphasized.

*Is There a Written Record of How the Nursing Quality Assurance Program Achieves Standards?* The best way to illustrate that standards are met is to review each standard and its required characteristics and to write a brief description of how the program has complied with each. Also helpful is to include copies of audits, clinical research studies, or progress reports to clarify documentation further. A written record allows the committee and appropriate staff members (as well as accreditation surveyors) to see how the program works and where to look for clarification. This record should be ongoing and updated at least quarterly. Also, the Joint Commission publishes a questionnaire to help institutions prepare for accreditation. It would be wise to maintain a file of current questionnaires as they become available.

*When Should Preparation Start for an Accreditation Visit?* Preparation for an accreditation visit should start the day after the previous visit has ended. Most facilities wait until the last possible moment to begin preparation. "We are too busy; we are already in compliance; there is not that much difference in the updated standards. . ." are just a few of the most frequently given excuses for procrastinating.

This usually results in a panic-stricken rush, with personnel working long hours and instituting last-minute studies and everyone feeling anxious and ill-prepared. Remember, quality assurance is a constant process designed to improve patient care. By developing a system that provides constant monitoring and well-documented evaluation, accreditation visits will achieve their original purpose—to provide a learning experience for the benefit of staff and patients alike.

## COMMISSION ON ACCREDITATION OF REHABILITATION FACILITIES

### Historical Background

The Commission on Accreditation of Rehabilitation Facilities (CARF) is a "private non-profit organization established by and for the field of rehabilitation and habilitation to adopt and apply standards in organizations throughout the nation."[15] The organization was formed in 1966 by the Association of Rehabilitation Centers and the National Association of Sheltered Workshops and Homebound Programs. For nearly ten years prior to CARF's formation, these two associations had developed standards for organizations in their respective memberships. Once these separate sets of standards had been set, CARF was established to unify these standards and to improve the quality of services being provided in the organizations. CARF was also seen as a means of informing the public:

> that accredited organizations had earned this recognition through their provision of consistently high quality services to people with disabilities as assessed by a competent, independent, voluntary authority.[16]

A few of the key benefits of CARF accreditation include:*

- The Commission's national standards set a common level of program expectations and performance.
- The Commission possesses a level of credibility in making impartial judgment concerning organizations' efficiency and effectiveness and provides for an ongoing system of total organization monitoring.
- Accreditation serves to define those organizations that have met national standards.

---

* This list of benefits is reprinted from *The CARF Story* with permission of Commission on Accreditation of Rehabilitation Facilities, undated.

- Accreditation offers a legitimate accountability mechanism reflective of but independent from the delivery system.
- Accreditation offers the opportunity for an educational and consultative process geared around program improvement.
- The Commission's accreditation offers a confidence to consumers that a monitoring system that is concerned with their best interests is in place.
- CARF accreditation is a mechanism that can be used equally by government, consumers, providers, professional organizations, educators, and various funding sources.[17]

The numerous advantages of CARF accreditation mandate that any rehabilitation nursing quality assurance system comply with its standards. A set of "test questions" (similar to the preceding Joint Commission questions on compliance) will help the nursing quality assurance chairperson adequately prepare for a CARF survey.

## CARF Standard Compliance*

*Does the Nursing Quality Assurance Chairperson Have the Latest CARF Accreditation Manual?* When preparing for any accreditation visit, it is essential to possess the latest standards manual. As previously described in the section on Joint Commission compliance, the nursing quality assurance chairperson must have quick and easy access to the most recent CARF accreditation information as well as to any updating information sent to the facility.

*Is the Chairperson Thoroughly Familiar with the "Program Evaluation" Section in the CARF Manual?* Unlike the Joint Commission manual, there is no component specifically labeled "Quality Assurance." Instead, those guidelines for evaluating care are presented in "Guidelines and Specifications for Program Evaluation."[18] CARF's definition of program evaluation is similar to definitions of quality assurance previously described in this chapter.

Program evaluation, as defined by the Commission, is a systematic procedure for determining the effectiveness and efficiency with which results following rehabilitation services are achieved by persons served. These results are collected on a regular continuous basis rather than through periodic sampling. The underlying principle of this definition is

* These standards are reprinted from *Standards Manual, 1987,* with permission of Commission on Accreditation of Rehabilitation Facilities, © 1987.

results; that is, the organization's evaluation system should be able to identify the results of service and the effect of the program on individuals served. From this, program performance can be improved and community support can be enhanced.[19]

As would be expected from a rehabilitation organization, the emphasis is on program goals and objectives and measurements of program efficiency. Additionally, the resulting data produced by the evaluation system "should be made available to decision makers as soon as possible after the close of a reporting period; also, it should be used by management to maintain or improve program performance."[20]

A major difference between Joint Commission and CARF quality assurance guidelines is that CARF program evaluation is interdisciplinary team-oriented. Program goals and objectives are *team*-specific rather than *discipline*-specific. The nursing quality assurance program must reflect and interrelate with the quality assurance monitors developed by each team (i.e., spinal cord injury team, stroke team, and so forth). (If the rehabilitation unit is located within an acute care facility, the chairperson must rely on the representative from the rehabilitation unit to provide needed expertise. Succeeding chapters will delineate more specifically the role of rehabilitation representatives when the unit is housed within an acute care hospital.)

CARF has published a number of informative examples on development of program evaluation. These are obtainable for a small fee by contacting CARF headquarters. As preparations for accreditation progress, the chairperson should feel free to call the appropriate accrediting organization if questions or concerns arise. Personnel are willing and eager to facilitate an organization's attempts to improve its health care services.

*Is the Facility Seeking To Accredit Individual Programs? If So, Is the Nursing Quality Assurance Chairperson Familiar with Each Program's Requirements?* In addition to comprehensive inpatient rehabilitation services, CARF offers accreditation for a number of individual programs (e.g., spinal cord injury, chronic pain management, brain injury, outpatient).[21] Each program has specific requirements to fulfill. Although the program manager or coordinator maintains the responsibility for meeting established standards, the nursing quality assurance chairperson is responsible for ensuring that the quality-of-care monitors reflect nursing's effectiveness as team members. As such he or she must be thoroughly aware of each program's standards.

The preceding questions should alert the chairperson to CARF requirements that are different in emphasis from those of the Joint Commission. Additionally, certain key points should be considered by the chairperson when preparing for any accreditation visit. These were explained in detail in the section on the Joint

Commission and are simply summarized at this point. The nursing quality assurance chairperson should

- have access to the latest CARF publications, newsletters, and bulletins
- maintain a written record of how the nursing quality assurance program contributes to successful program evaluation
- develop and maintain a system of monitoring and evaluation that is continually updated according to hospital and accrediting bodies' standards

## PROFESSIONAL NURSING ORGANIZATIONS

A profession's professional organizations have an enormous impact on standard development and resulting quality assurance issues. The organizations that are recognized as representative of the professional practice of nursing are utilized as role models, resources, consultants, and educational experts in organizing nursing practice in all settings. The American Nurses' Association and the Association of Rehabilitation Nurses are the two professional nursing organizations that have the greatest influence on rehabilitation nursing.

### American Nurses' Association

The American Nurses' Association (ANA), the professional society for nursing in the United States, is "responsible for defining nursing, establishing the scope of practice, and setting standards for professional nursing practice."[22] These responsibilities led to the evolution of standards of practice utilized to formulate quality assurance programs.

In 1966, the ANA formed nursing practice divisions, each of which developed nursing practice standards. The publication that set the generic standards for the profession of nursing was *Standards of Nursing Practice*.[23] Published in 1973, these standards provide direction for evaluating quality of care. The need for formal, documented methods of determining quality care led the ANA to publish its statement on quality assurance. A 1975 document, *A Plan for the Implementation of the Standards of Nursing Practice*, also included a plan for implementation of standards of nursing practice. The ANA's plan emphasizes determining the degree to which standards are met by securing appropriate measurements and introducing change to improve quality of care.[24]

The nursing quality assurance chairperson should maintain a copy of the ANA generic standards as well as the Association's model of quality assurance. These references will correlate with the standards for rehabilitation nursing developed jointly by the ANA and the Association of Rehabilitation Nurses.

**Association of Rehabilitation Nurses**

The Association of Rehabilitation Nurses (ARN) is an international organization founded in 1974 to enhance the quality of rehabilitation nursing service. It is the representative organization for professional rehabilitation nurses. In 1977, ARN and ANA worked together to publish *Standards of Rehabilitation Nursing Practice*.[25] These standards were revised in 1986 to reflect the continued evolution of rehabilitation nursing practice.[26]

The 1986 revision defines a standard as:

> a norm that expresses an agreed-upon level of practice that has been developed to characterize, measure, and provide guidance for achieving excellence.[27]

The standards of rehabilitation nursing are based on the use of the nursing process in the nurse-patient relationship. Quality assurance is monitored as described in Standard VIII—"Quality Assurance":

> The nurse participates in peer review and interdisciplinary program evaluation to assure that high quality nursing care is provided to individuals in a rehabilitation setting.[28]

As in previous quality assurance standards and definitions, the emphasis is on mandating quality care. The rehabilitation specialty also highlights the importance of peer review in an interdisciplinary collaborative setting. The nursing quality assurance chairperson must maintain the specialty's standards of practice and incorporate them into the system of evaluating quality of care.

**SUMMARY**

The nursing profession is governed by a variety of standards, including both internal and external regulatory measures. The nursing quality assurance committee must familiarize itself with the norms that guide nursing practice. Of particular importance to rehabilitation nursing are the standards of the Joint Commission, CARF, ANA, and ARN.

A careful review of these standards shows that the bases for nursing quality assurance guidelines are similar in all organizations. Rehabilitation specialists must pay particular attention to the need for interdisciplinary collaboration when applying standards, but the quality assurance committee should find a pleasing symmetry in the organizations' descriptions of quality assurance issues.

Successful accreditation surveys depend on the nursing quality assurance chairperson's ability to maintain an ongoing, well-documented system of monitoring and evaluating the quality of care provided. Utilizing the most up-to-date information provided by accrediting bodies and professional organizations will help the nursing quality assurance committee to develop a plan that meets the unique needs of rehabilitation nursing.

## NOTES

1. Philip Babcock Gove, ed., *Webster's Third New International Dictionary* (Springfield, Mass.: Merriam-Webster, Inc., 1981), 2223.

2. Joint Commission on Accreditation of Healthcare Organizations, *Accreditation Manual for Hospitals—1970* [Updated 1973] (Chicago: Joint Commission on Accreditation of Healthcare Organizations, 1973), 1.

3. Ibid., 1–2.

4. Ibid., 2.

5. Ibid., 1.

6. Christina M. Mumma, ed., *Rehabilitation Nursing: Concepts and Practice—A Core Curriculum*, 2nd ed. (Evanston, Ill.: Rehabilitation Nursing Foundation, 1987), 459.

7. Maryland Hospital Association, letter distributed to board of trustees, chief executive officers, and Maryland Hospital Association member institutions regarding quality leadership assembly meeting; letter dated December 22, 1987, 1–2.

8. Ibid., 2.

9. Joint Commission on Accreditation of Healthcare Oraganizations, *Accreditation Manual for Hospitals/88* (Chicago: Joint Commission on Accreditation of Healthcare Organizations, 1987), 235.

10. Ibid., 149.

11. Ibid., 148–150.

12. Ibid., 193.

13. Ibid., 206.

14. Ibid., 201.

15. Commission on Accreditation of Rehabilitation Facilities, *The CARF Story* (undated pamphlet) (Tucson, Ariz.: Commission on Accreditation of Rehabilitation Facilities), 1.

16. Ibid.

17. Ibid., 5–6.

18. Commission on Accreditation of Rehabilitation Facilities, "Guidelines and Specifications for Program Evaluation," in *Standards Manual, 1987* (Tucson, Ariz.: Commission on Accreditation of Rehabilitation Facilities, 1987), 137–144.

19. Ibid., 137.

20. Ibid., 143.

21. Ibid., 43–100.

22. American Nurses' Association and Association of Rehabilitation Nurses, *Standards of Rehabilitation Nursing Practice* (Kansas City, Mo.: American Nurses' Association, 1986), 1.

23. American Nurses' Association, *Standards of Nursing Practice* (Kansas City, Mo.: American Nurses' Association, 1973), 1–5.

24. American Nurses' Association, *A Plan for the Implementation of the Standards of Nursing*

*Practice* (Kansas City, Mo.: American Nurses' Association, 1975), 1–4.

25. American Nurses' Association and Association of Rehabilitation Nurses, *Standards of Rehabilitation Nursing Practice* (Kansas City, Mo.: American Nurses' Association, 1977), 1.

26. American Nurses' Association and Association of Rehabilitation Nurses, *Standards of Rehabilitation Nursing Practice*, 1–2.

27. Ibid., 13.

28. Ibid., 11.

---

## BIBLIOGRAPHY

American Nurses' Association. *A Plan for the Implementation of the Standards of Nursing Practice.* Kansas City, Mo.: American Nurses' Association, 1975.

American Nurses' Association. *Nursing: A Social Policy Statement.* Kansas City, Mo.: American Nurses' Association, 1980.

Calloway, Sue Dill. *Nursing and the Law.* Eau Claire, Wisc.: Professional Education Systems, 1986.

Cantor, Marjorie Moore. *Achieving Nursing Care Standards: Internal and External.* Rockville, Md.: Aspen Publishers, Inc., 1978.

Carter, Joan H.; Hilliard, Mildred; Castles, Mary Reardon; Stoll, Leona D.; and Cowan, Anne. *Standards of Nursing Care: A Guide for Evaluation.* New York: Springer, 1976.

Donabedian, Avedis. "Quality Assurance." *Journal of Gerontological Nursing* 44 (1966): 166, 206.

Donabedian, Avedis. *The Criteria and Standards of Quality.* Ann Arbor, Mich.: Health Administration Press, 1982.

Graham, Nancy O., ed. *Quality Assurance in Hospitals.* Rockville, Md.: Aspen Publishers, Inc., 1982.

Maloof, Malcom. "Preparing for Agency Accreditation." *Rehabilitation Nursing* 11 (1986): 11–12.

Mason, Elizabeth. *How To Write Meaningful Nursing Standards.* New York: John Wiley & Sons, Inc., 1978.

Mayer, Marlene G.; Norby, Ronald B.; and Watson, Annita B. *Quality Assurance for Patient Care: Nursing Perspectives.* New York: Appleton-Century-Crofts, 1977.

McClellan, Marilyn G. "Toward Clinical Excellence in Nursing: A Program for Development of Nurses." *Nursing Administration Quarterly* 6 (1981): 26–29.

McClure, Margaret L. "The Long Road to Accountability." *Nursing Outlook* 26 (1978): 47–50.

Meisenheimer, Claire Gavin. "Incorporating JCAH Standards into a Quality Assurance Program." *Nursing Administration Quarterly* (Spring 1983): 1–8.

Nicholls, Marian E., and Wessells, Virginia G., eds. *Nursing Standards and Nursing Process.* Wakefield, Mass.: Contemporary Publishing, 1977.

Puetz, Belinda E., and Peters, Faye L. *Continuing Education for Nurses: A Complete Guide to Effective Programs.* Rockville, Md.: Aspen Publishers, Inc., 1985.

Rowland, Howard S., and Rowland, Beatrice L., eds. *Nursing Administration Handbook.* 2nd ed. Rockville, Md.: Aspen Publishers, Inc., 1985.

Thompson, Teresa C. "A Proactive Approach to Accrediting Standards." *Rehabilitation Nursing* 11 (1986): 8–10.

---

## SUGGESTED READINGS

American Nurses' Association. *Standards of Nursing Practice.* Kansas City, Mo.: American Nurses' Association, 1973.

American Nurses' Association. *A Plan for the Implementation of the Standards of Nursing Practice.* Kansas City, Mo.: American Nurses' Association, 1975.

American Nurses' Association. *Code for Nurses with Interpretive Statements.* Kansas City, Mo.: American Nurses' Association, 1980.

American Nurses' Association. *Nursing: A Social Policy Statement.* Kansas City, Mo.: American Nurses' Association, 1980.

American Nurses' Association and Association of Rehabilitation Nurses. *Standards of Rehabilitation Nursing Practice.* Kansas City, Mo.: American Nurses' Association, 1986.

Bloch, Doris. "Criteria, Standards, Norms—Crucial Terms in Quality Assurance." *Journal of Nursing Administration* 7 (1977): 20–30.

Broun, Barbara J., ed. "Quality Assurance and Peer Review." *Nursing Administration Quarterly* 1 (1977): 1–145.

Broun, Barbara J., ed. "Quality Assurance Update." *Nursing Administration Quarterly* 7 (1983): 1–93.

Cantor, Marjorie Moore. *Achieving Nursing Care Standards: Internal and External.* Rockville, Md.: Aspen Publishers, Inc., 1978.

Carter, Joan H., and Hilliard, Mildred. *Standards of Nursing Care.* New York: Springer, 1972.

Carter, Joan H.; Hilliard, Mildred; Castles, Mary Reardon; Stoll, Leona D.; and Cowan, Anne. *Standards of Nursing Care: A Guide for Evaluation.* New York: Springer, 1976.

Donabedian, Avedis. *The Definition of Quality and Approaches to Its Assessment.* Ann Arbor, Mich.: Health Administration Press, 1980.

Donabedian, Avedis. *The Criteria and Standards of Quality.* Ann Arbor, Mich.: Health Administration Press, 1982.

Donabedian, Avedis; Wheeler, John R.C.; and Wysqewianski, Leon. "An Integrative Model of Quality, Cost, and Health." In *Hospital Quality Assurance*, edited by Jesus J. Pena, Alden N. Haffner, Bernard Rosen, and Donald W. Light. Rockville, Md.: Aspen Publishers, Inc., 1984.

Froebe, Doris J., and Bain, R. Joyce. *Quality Assurance Programs and Controls in Nursing.* St. Louis, Mo.: C.V. Mosby Co., 1976.

Graham, Nancy O., ed. *Quality Assurance in Hospitals.* Rockville, Md.: Aspen Publishers, Inc., 1982.

Greer, Scott. "Introduction: Professional Standards Review Organization." In *Proceedings: Conference Professional Self-Regulation*, edited by Health Resources Administration. Washington, D.C.: Department of Health, Education, and Welfare, 1975.

Harmon, Carol A. "Involving Staff in Nursing Quality Assurance." *Quality Review Bulletin* 6 (1980): 26–30.

Hegedus, Kathryn Stewart. "A Patient Outcome Criterion Measure." *Supervisor Nurse* 10 (1979): 40–45.

Horn, Barbara J., and Swain, Mary Ann. *Development of Criterion Measures of Nursing Care.* Springfield, Va.: National Technical Information Service, 1977.

InterQual. *Advanced Nursing Audit Seminar Manual.* Chicago: InterQual, 1977.

Lang, Norma M. "Quality Assurance in Nursing." *AORN Journal* 22 (1975): 180–186.

Lesnik, Milton V., and Anderson, Bernice E. *Nursing Practice and the Law.* Philadelphia: J.B. Lippincott, 1955.

Lieske, Anna Marie. "Standards: The Basis of a Quality Assurance Program." In *Quality Assurance—A Complete Guide to Effective Programs*, edited by Claire Gavin Meisenheimer. Rockville, Md.: Aspen Publishers, Inc., 1985.

Luke, Roice D.; Krueger, Janelle C.; and Modrow, Robert E. *Organization and Change in Health Care Quality Assurance*. Rockville, Md.: Aspen Publishers, Inc., 1983.

Mason, Elizabeth. *How To Write Meaningful Nursing Standards*. New York: John Wiley & Sons, Inc., 1978.

Mayer, Marlene G.; Norby, Ronald B.; and Watson, Annita B. *Quality Assurance for Patient Care: Nursing Perspectives*. New York: Appleton-Century-Crofts, 1977.

Meisenheimer, Claire Gavin, ed. *Quality Assurance—A Complete Guide to Effective Programs*. Rockville, Md.: Aspen Publishers, Inc., 1985.

Nicholls, Marion E., and Wessells, Virginia G., eds. *Nursing Standards and Nursing Process*. Wakefield, Mass.: Contemporary Publishing, 1977.

Nightingale, Florence. *Notes on Nursing: What It Is and What It Is Not*. New York: Dover Publications, 1969.

Orlando, Ida Jean. *The Dynamic Nurse-Patient Relationship*. New York: G.P. Putman's Sons, 1961.

Pena, Jesus J.; Haffner, Alden N.; Rosen, Bernard; and Light, Donald W., eds. *Hospital Quality Assurance: Risk Management and Program Evaluation*. Rockville, Md.: Aspen Publishers, Inc., 1984.

Phaneuf, Maria C. *The Nursing Audit and Self-Regulation in Nursing Practice*. New York: Appleton-Century-Crofts, 1976.

Phaneuf, Maria C., and Wandelt, Mabel A. "Quality Assurance in Nursing." *Nursing Forum* 13 (1974): 328–345.

Phaneuf, Maria C., and Wandelt, Mabel A. "Letters." *Quality Review Bulletin* 7 (1981): 8.

Phaneuf, Maria C., and Wandelt, Mabel A. "Obstacles to and Potentials for Nursing Quality Appraisal." *Quality Review Bulletin* 7 (1981): 2–5.

Prescott, Patricia. "Evaluation Research: Issues in Evaluation of Nursing Programs." *Nursing Administration Quarterly* 2 (1978): 63–80.

Schmied, Elsie. "Living with Cost Containment." *Journal of Nursing Administration* 10 (1980): 1147.

Subcommittee on Standards, Section on Nursing, American Thoracic Society. "Development of Nursing Standards." *American Thoracic Society News* 4 (1978): 10–11.

Watson, Annita, and Mayers, Marlene. "Evaluating the Quality of Patient Care through Retrospective Chart Review." *Journal of Nursing Administration* 6, no. 2 (1976): 17–21.

Weiss, Carol H. *Evaluation Research: Methods of Assessing Program Effectiveness*. Englewood Cliffs, N.J.: Prentice-Hall, Inc., 1972.

Woody, Mary F. "An Evaluator's Perspective." *Nursing Research* 29 (1980): 74–77.

Zimmer, Marie J. "A Model for Evaluating Nursing Care." *Hospitals* 48 (1974): 91–95, 131.

Zimmer, Marie J., guest ed. "Quality Assurance." *Nursing Clinics of North America* 9 (1974).

# Chapter 3

# Developing a Nursing Quality Assurance Program: Assessment and Planning

## INTRODUCTION

Any process that serves to evaluate with the intent to improve nursing care is nursing quality assurance. The nursing quality assurance committee, in conjunction with the chief nursing administrator, provides the direction for the department's quality assurance activities. Committee responsibilities include

- identification and/or review of nursing department standards that describe the desired and achievable level of rehabilitation nursing practice
- determination of standard-based criteria that are objective, measurable, and reliable indicators of patient care
- collection of data to measure degree of standard attainment
- analysis of data to identify problems and to determine strengths and weaknesses
- identification of appropriate actions to maintain and/or improve rehabilitation nursing care
- documentation of all nursing quality assurance activities, including process, data interpretation, actions taken, and impact on nursing practice

Although the nursing quality assurance committee assumes the responsibility for overseeing program implementation, each and every member of the nursing department retains the accountability for providing quality care. Therefore, the entire nursing department should be involved in implementing a quality assurance program.

## NURSING QUALITY ASSURANCE STRATEGIES

There are two major formats for the development of nursing quality assurance programs: facility-based and unit-based. Facility-based programs are founded on

31

standards that are generic across all services.[1] Such standards allow for monitoring and evaluation across disciplines, i.e., "increase in ability to independently perform activities of daily living."

Facility-based data provide the interdisciplinary rehabilitation team with overall program trends and information concerning program effectiveness. Resources for the collection of facility-based data include risk management, infection control, utilization management, medical records, and functional status measurements.

Unit-based programs evolve from standards that are specific to patients on a particular unit. Monitoring is developed based on direct caregiver input and reviewed by additional clinical resources such as the unit manager or the clinical nurse specialist.[2] Unit quality assurance activities are chaired by a registered nurse who has expertise in quality assurance, i.e., the nurse manager. Unit staff members, in collaboration with clinical resources, collect data, discuss trends, identify problems, and recommend action to improve nursing care.

A successful rehabilitation quality assurance program encompasses facets of both formats. According to data from the National Association of Rehabilitation Facilities (June 1987), the average free-standing rehabilitation facility has fewer than 100 beds.[3] This size facility is small enough to allow adequate interdisciplinary communication for the identification of generic "across-service" standards. Simultaneously, unit-based standards that concentrate on specific patient groups (e.g., stroke, spinal cord-injured) can be developed. This will foster specific nurse accountability for patient care by directly involving the staff nurse in the monitoring and evaluation process. Regardless of design strategies, an appropriate rehabilitation nursing quality assurance program must be developed if both the specialty and its nursing practice are to be strengthened.


## PROGRAM DESIGN

Whether implementing a new program or revising an established system, it is necessary to review the overall picture of quality assurance needs as they exist in each rehabilitation facility or unit. The following outline is intended as a guide to thorough needs assessment and program planning.

I.   Assessment.
     A. *Data collection.* The following resources should be utilized to gather
        pertinent data:
        1. Risk management. Successful risk management involves the identification and analysis of potential risks and the development of preventive measures to reduce or eliminate them. Particularly important

statistics for rehabilitation nursing quality assurance may include the incidence and evaluation of

a) Falls. In rehabilitation, the concept of independence is continually promoted. With independence, however, comes an increased risk of falls. Factors to note when monitoring falls include (1) the patient's diagnosis, age, sex, orientation status, and activity level; (2) the time of day, day of week, and location of the incident; (3) medications taken that may have contributed to the fall; and (4) length of stay at time of the fall. Carefully categorizing falls may help to clarify their occurrence. Possible subdivisions include: falls, attended (staff member present); falls, unattended (no witness to the fall); and lowered to floor (patient was eased to the floor by a staff member during transfer or ambulation to avoid an uncontrolled fall). A precise method of monitoring falls should help to decrease risk factors in a rehabilitation setting while continuing to promote independence.

b) Pressure sore development. Many rehabilitation patients experience a decrease in mobility that may or may not be permanent. With immobility comes the risk of impaired skin integrity. The nursing quality assurance committee must monitor not only pressure sore development after admission to the rehabilitation facility or unit, but the rate of healing as well. The effectiveness of treatment may be measured by the rapidity with which a pressure sore heals. The rate of healing for patients admitted with preexisting skin impairment is also an important monitor. The patient's age, sex, diagnosis, and degree of immobility should be noted.

c) Fecal impaction. Compromised bowel status is a frequently occurring rehabilitation problem. Neurological injury, trauma, chronic pain, and progressive neuromuscular diseases are some of the conditions that influence bowel functioning. A fecal impaction results from failure to initiate and/or maintain an appropriate bowel regimen. The presence of an impaction, as well as measures to eliminate one (i.e., manual removal or enemas) may pose a serious threat to life. Fecal impaction may trigger an episode of autonomic dysreflexia in a patient with spinal cord injury; manual removal may compromise a patient's cardiac or cerebrovascular status. Data obtained from monitoring this problem should be used to evaluate bowel retraining methods throughout the rehabilitation facility or unit. Factors to note for monitoring include the patient's age, sex, diagnosis, activity level, diet, unit location, length of stay at time of impaction development, and treatment interventions.

d) Unscheduled transfer of patients to acute care hospitals. Becoming increasingly important to all rehabilitation specialists are the reasons necessitating the unscheduled transfer of patients to the acute care sector. As previously mentioned, DRG constraints may result in the admission of "quicker and sicker" rehabilitation patients. Conditions (e.g., pulmonary emboli, deteriorating neurological status) that result in acute medical instability may be anticipated and even avoided by initiating appropriate preventive measures. In addition to the demographic characteristics of age, sex, diagnosis, activity level, medical reason for transfer, length of stay, and the referring source (if the patient was in an acute care facility or at home prior to admission to rehabilitation) should be monitored. It is important to note any trends in transfer and the patient's referral source. Certain acute care personnel may need education regarding a patient's readiness and physical ability to participate in a rehabilitation program, as may referring home health practitioners.

e) Incidents occurring during therapeutic home visits. Therapeutic home visits are part of almost every patient's rehabilitation program. Home visits, whether of several hours or several days, serve as a means of gauging the patient/family's ability to adapt to altered roles and carry out new means of performing activities of daily living. Such visits may also indicate the success of a rehabilitation program. It is important to know the exact nature of the incident (i.e., a fall or failure to take medications properly) and the day, time, and location of the incident. Such monitoring will help the staff to assess readiness for discharge and the adequacy of existing patient education programs.

f) Medication errors. Monitoring medication errors is important to all nursing departments, regardless of specialty. In rehabilitation, however, the patient often plays a key role in medication distribution. Many rehabilitation facilities/units have self-medication programs by which the patient learns to assume responsibility for his or her medication regimen. The definition of medication errors may be expanded to include patient error as well. This type of error would be especially evident during therapeutic home visits.

2. Utilization review. Utilization review is the process of evaluating the use of health care services and facilities against preestablished criteria. Pertinent rehabilitation data to retrieve include

a) Lengths of stay of specialty programs. Rehabilitation facilities often consist of two or more units that house a specific patient population (e.g., spinal cord-injured, head-injured, stroke). The Commission on Accreditation of Rehabilitation Facilities (CARF) offers individual accreditation to a variety of individual specialty programs. The facility that can offer the shortest length of stay and the most cost-effective programs, while providing measurable rehabilitation gains, not only will attract patients but will show considerable financial gains as well. Quality assurance should monitor lengths of stay in regard to cost-effectiveness and patient outcomes.

    *b*) Admission appropriateness. All rehabilitation facilities/units should have clearly defined admission criteria based on the patient population served. Examples of criteria include medical stability, specific length of time from injury/illness to request for rehabilitation services, and gauging cognitive and physical ability to participate in a rehabilitation program. Monitoring admission appropriateness in conjunction with patient outcomes may help to clarify admission criteria as well as appropriateness of admissions.

    *c*) Definitions of functional status measures. In contrast to acute care, rehabilitative care is based on descriptions of function rather than etiology-specific diagnostic categories.[4] Using functional status measures instead of, or in addition to, diagnostic descriptions is not a new rehabilitation concept, but it is one that lacks testing in reliability and validity. Although there are measurement tools available, the rehabilitation specialty does not have precise, universal definitions of functional status. In order for one rehabilitation facility to discuss functional status with another, the individual status definitions must be shared and understood. Utilization review, by evaluating services based on preestablished criteria, can contribute to the development of definitions of functional status descriptors. Quality assurance, by monitoring outcome status based on functional status criteria, can also contribute to a system of evaluating care based on objective measurements.

3. Infection control. Trends in both nosocomial and community-acquired infections must be noted. Examples of items especially important for the rehabilitation nursing quality assurance committee to monitor are

    *a*) Incidence of urinary tract infection. Compromised bladder status is a common problem for rehabilitation patients. Recognizing this, rehabilitation nurses should initiate appropriate preventive and monitoring measures. Occurrences of nosocomial urinary tract infections may indicate ineffectiveness of bladder training programs or patient education. Tracking urinary tract infections should involve patient demographic data (age, sex, diagnosis), treatment regimens, and patient education programs. Particularly important is whether the patient has an indwelling catheter or is on an intermittent catheterization program.

b) Wound site infections. Multiple trauma and orthopedic patients are just two examples of rehabilitation clients who are at risk of wound infection. Monitoring the incidence of nosocomial wound infections should provide data on treatment regimens, patient participation in treatment, patient education, and whether any of the patient's roommates are suffering from an infectious process.

c) Preadmission infections (community-acquired). Monitoring infections present upon the patient's admission is important in identifying trends and in determining treatment and educational needs.

4. Hospital quality assurance. As the department responsible for monitoring the effectiveness of hospitalwide services, the hospital quality assurance committee may serve as a resource for the retrieval of

a) Program evaluation. Program evaluation is based on interdisciplinary team collaboration. Goals and objectives are team-oriented and not discipline-oriented. Each program (e.g., stroke, pain management) should have established its own criteria for success. Hospital quality assurance could serve as the coordinator for data collection regarding outcome measurements. Nursing quality assurance would be provided with information on criteria achievement. For example, if the stroke team has established an outcome criterion that "upon discharge, 90 percent of stroke patients will be continent of bowel and bladder," the percentage of achievement could be analyzed by the nursing quality assurance committee. Nursing's role in the success of this criterion would be reviewed and evaluated and, if needed, recommendations for improvement made.

b) Interdisciplinary team functioning. In no other specialty is the patient's treatment program so dependent on successful interdisciplinary team functioning. The hospital quality assurance committee may serve as both a means of monitoring interdisciplinary communication and a "sounding board" for team concerns. Representatives from all disciplines should serve on the committee. With appropriate representation, both intra- and interteam problems and strengths could be shared, evaluated, and acted upon.

c) Patient/family concerns. The occurrences, evaluation, and resolution of patient/family concerns should be monitored on a regular basis. Patient/family satisfaction surveys may be performed at discharge or as a follow up at a specified length of time after discharge. Some facilities may choose to assess formally (written) satisfaction throughout hospitalization. Obviously, patient/family concerns are continually monitored either verbally or by written communications. Regardless of communication method, patient/family concerns should be monitored by the hospital quality assurance committee. This information is also invaluable to the nursing quality assurance committee. By tracking the type of concern, who (patient or family) brought it to the staff's attention, staff identified in the concern, and the course of the patient's rehabilitation program, recommendations for improving patient care may be made with feedback to the patient and family.

5. Nursing administration. Administrative data that help to illustrate the effectiveness of patient care are:

   a) Patient classification system. A patient classification (or patient acuity) system can be defined as "the systematic identification and assessment of the individualized nursing care requirements of a group of patients."[5] The nursing quality assurance committee should monitor patient acuity, staffing adequacy ratio, and correlation between staffing adequacy ratio and adverse patient occurrences.

   b) Staff certification. In addition to mandatory licensure, there are a wide variety of certification options available to registered nurses. In rehabilitation, the Association of Rehabilitation Nurses has developed a certification examination to recognize those nurses who are experts in the field of rehabilitation nursing. The title Certified Rehabilitation Registered Nurse (CRRN) is awarded upon successful completion of the examination. The number of certified nurses in a facility is important when monitoring professional recognition of expertise as well as the personal motivation of the nurses who successfully pass the examination. This monitoring should not be limited to recognized clinical experts (CRRNs), but may include credentialing in administration, infection control, quality assurance, or other appropriate certifications.

   c) Criteria-based job descriptions and performance evaluations. Job descriptions should be based on measurable outcome criteria so that employee and employer have a clear understanding of responsibilities and expectations. Performance evaluations based on criteria achievement provide an objective method of assessing job performance. Nursing administration and nursing quality assurance should work together to monitor the job descriptions, relevance of outcome criteria, and methods of performance evaluation.

6. Unit nurse managers/unit representatives. Nurse managers and the individual unit representatives may collect the following information.

   a) Timeliness of nursing documentation. The nursing department's standards for completion of certain facets of documentation should be carefully monitored. Are admission assessments completed within identified time frames? Are nursing care plans completed in a timely fashion? In rehabilitation facilities interdisciplinary assessments are common. Is nursing's participation in such assessments timely and accurate? Are discharge summaries pertinent and finished on time? Are nursing follow-up interventions conducted within specified time frames (i.e., follow-up phone calls, home visits, participation in outpatient return appointments)?

   b) Thoroughness of nursing documentation. In rehabilitation, nursing documentation is often geared to the patient's progress in specific areas of his or her rehabilitation program. Standards for documentation should be designed around the philosophy and interventions of rehabilitation nursing. Nursing quality assurance should assist in the development and evaluation of charting standards. In addition to monitoring adherence to department standards, the committee should note compliance with legal principles and individual program standards.

   c) Patient education programs. Patient education is an integral component of any rehabilitation endeavor. Documentation of the objectives, content, patient participation, and teaching outcomes should be monitored. A system for evaluation of the program's effectiveness should be in place and monitored by unit staff as well as the nursing quality assurance committee.

7. Staff development. Professionals must pursue education so that they are up to date and knowledgeable in their particular areas of expertise. Professional accountability includes the responsibility of keeping abreast of the changes and developments in the health care field. The nursing department's education specialists can be a valuable resource for the nursing quality assurance committee.

   a) Educational program attendance. Educational requirements should be part of the standards of any nursing department. Mandatory programs should include not only cardiopulmonary resuscitation, infection control, and safety issues but programs specific to rehabilitation as well. Current developments in specific areas of rehabilitation (e.g., spinal cord injury or head injury) may be part of unit-specific programs presented on a regular basis. If the facility/unit utilizes a specific method of transfer and positioning of patients (Bobath principles, for example), mandatory refresher courses could be a component of staff development. Attendance at a minimal number of both inservices and outside programs should be established to help promote educational accountability. The staff development department is responsible for providing programs and assisting personnel to identify appropriate sources of outside programs as well. Nursing quality assurance issues include adherence to attendance standards, provision of adequate educational opportunities, and evaluation of education programs' effectiveness and impact on staff.

> *b)* Staff presentation of educational programs. The nursing staff should be active participants in not only patient/family education but staff development as well. The staff will appreciate the opportunity to share knowledge with colleagues and to network. Nursing quality assurance could monitor issues similar to those identified under "educational program attendance" but from the viewpoint of the nursing staff presenting the educational information.

The nursing quality assurance chairperson must see to it that data gathered determine the degree to which standards are met and help to introduce changes aimed at improving patient care. Whether the sources of collected data are used to analyze facility or unit-based services, patient care must be evaluated on measurable criteria. Only after the collection of pertinent data can monitors be developed to measure outcomes. How do the chairperson and the committee identify which of the incoming data are most critical?

B. *Evaluation of collected data.*
  1. The program's foundation must be based on applicable standards. (Details of standards and determining compliance are presented in Chapter 2.)
     *a)* Are data sufficient in both quantity and quality to measure compliance with the Joint Commission, CARF, and nursing practice standards?
     *b)* Does the facility house individually CARF-accredited specialty programs (i.e., spinal cord injury, head injury, pain management, or outpatient department)? If so, are there adequate sources of data to determine whether the specialty requirements have been met?

    *c)* Has the nursing quality assurance committee reviewed the hospital's mission and philosophy statements as well as those of the department of nursing? These statements will identify the hospital's major purpose and what aspects of care are most emphasized. The chairperson, in turn, must ensure that the data collected will provide objective, measurable, and relevant facts about patient care.

2. The program must internalize both explicit and implicit values of the facility and the department of nursing.

    *a)* Values, those attributes that are indispensable for practice, are interpretations of quality.[6]

    *b)* Explicit values may be identified from philosophy and standards. Implicit values are identified through practice and experience. For example, if research is a highly valued concept, the chairperson must take care to gather data with which to formulate clinical research projects. If professional continuing education is emphasized, appropriate data must be furnished from the nursing education department.

3. The chairperson must utilize both experience and instinct to develop a successful nursing quality assurance program.

    *a)* The chairperson must differentiate between a trend in data and isolated occurrences.

    *b)* Data should both indicate problem areas and provide support for successful nursing outcomes.

Once the chairperson and the committee have established the data that are relevant for the program, they are ready to plan the actual structure of the program.

II. Planning.
  A. *Goal.* The goal is to formulate an organized program that evaluates the effectiveness of rehabilitation nursing practice.
  B. *Format.* Exhibit 3-1 illustrates a sample format for the identification of quality assurance monitors.
    1. The "criteria" column is used to identify the criteria established to assess quality of health care delivery. There are three types of criteria: structure, process, and outcome.[7]
      *a)* Structure. Structure concerns physical, fiscal, and organizational settings. For example, all entranceways will be wide enough to facilitate wheelchair passage.
      *b)* Process. Process describes specific activities of the rehabilitation nurse. For example, nurse/patient collaborative rehabilitation

**Exhibit 3-1** Nursing Quality Assurance Monitors

| Criteria | Monitor | Standard of Acceptance | Method of Retrieval (including responsible party) |
|---|---|---|---|
| Nurse/patient collaborative goals will be documented within 48 hours of the patient's admission | Timeliness of nurse/patient collaboration on rehabilitation goal documentation | 100% compliance | Concurrent peer review of nursing documentation in medical record |

goals will be documented within 48 hours of the patient's admission.

    *c)* Outcome. Outcome indicates the end result of care by measuring a change in the patient's wellness. For example, patients with cerebrovascular accident will be continent of bladder functioning upon discharge.

2. The "monitor" column identifies the specific monitor used to indicate quality of services provided. For example, the documentation of timeliness of nurse/patient collaborative rehabilitation goals (process criteria) or the percentage of patients with cerebrovascular accident achieving bladder continence by discharge (outcome criteria).

3. The third column gives a standard of acceptance for the successful achievement of each criterion. The standard may be given in percentage form and/or in numerical form.

4. The fourth column, "method of retrieval," identifies where the data are gathered that measure the standard of acceptance. Examples include

    *a)* Survey

    *b)* Interview

    *c)* Questionnaire

    *d)* Observation

    *e)* Review of medical records: concurrent (occurring presently), retrospective (occurred in the past), or prospective (anticipated)

## ADEQUACY OF PROGRAM FORMAT

The following checklist should provide a guideline for evaluating the adequacy of an existing nursing quality assurance program or the plans for initiating one.

- What are the services of the nursing department that have the greatest impact on the quality of patient care? Are they facility-based or unit program-specific?

- Is there a written, comprehensive nursing quality assurance program? Is it integrated with the hospital quality assurance program? Who is responsible for the program?

- What is the process for quality assessment of patient care?

    1. Are monitors identified? Are they based on standards of care?

    2. Is there a problem identification/correction process?

    3. Do all levels of the nursing staff have the opportunity to identify problems and express concerns?

4. How often are data collected?

5. What methods are used—prospective, concurrent, retrospective, questionnaire, interview?

6. Who is responsible for collecting data?

7. What is the source of data? Is it representative of quality, quantity, and management?

8. What are the evaluation process and reporting method? Are monthly, quarterly, and/or annual reports given to the hospital quality assurance committee?

9. Are the reports shared with members of the nursing administrative team?

10. How are recommendations made for improving patient care?

11. Who has the authority to carry out recommendations?

12. Is there a method for evaluating the effectiveness of actions based on committee recommendations?

- Is the program cost-effective?

1. Are data used to assess the cost of program services?

2. Does information on staffing and patient acuity impact on nursing service costs? Are data contributing to evaluating the staffing adequacy ratio?

- Does the program meet requirements of accrediting agencies (the Joint Commission and CARF)?

- Is there a structured nursing quality assurance committee?

1. Are roles of members identified?

2. Are minutes and reports given to the medical staff, administration, and the governing body?

3. How are committee members chosen?

4. Who assumes responsibility for correlating the nursing quality assurance program with the hospital program?

5. Does the nursing administrator actively participate in the direction of quality assurance activities?

- Is there a monitoring system for staff credentialing?

1. Are job descriptions and performance evaluations based on standards?

2. Is there monitoring by peer review?

- Is research a component of the nursing quality assurance program?

1. How are research studies conducted?

2. How are the results of such studies used to improve patient care? How are the results shared with the nursing department?

3. Is information utilized to develop interdisciplinary research? How is this information shared with the rehabilitation team?

Appendix 3-A offers a sample rehabilitation nursing quality assurance plan. Any plan, however, is only as effective as the people who carry it out.

A key component of assessment and planning is analysis of the committee membership itself. The preceding guidelines are of value only if the committee members are successful in directing nursing quality assurance activities.

## COMMITTEE MEMBERSHIP

Committee memberships all too often consist of a small number of people who really want to be on a committee, compared with an unwilling majority who have been "volunteered" by their supervisors. The nursing quality assurance committee is no exception to this dilemma. However, an effective chairperson may be able to convince even the most reluctant of members that quality assurance is not only critical to the practice of nursing but an exciting concept as well. The following guidelines are meant to serve as a resource for committee selection. These suggestions consider both the free-standing rehabilitation facility and the rehabilitation unit located within an acute care facility.

### Chairperson

Fulfillment of the chairperson role is critical to the success of the nursing quality assurance program. A background in both nursing quality assurance and rehabilitation nursing is recommended. Although these notions may seem self-evident, it must be remembered that rehabilitation is a relatively new and rapidly growing specialty. Competition for experienced rehabilitation nurses is increasing. A nurse who has experience in both quality assurance and rehabilitation is not easy to find but is the ideal chairperson.

As previously noted, the average rehabilitation facility has fewer than 100 beds.[8] It is unlikely that a hospital of this size would hire a nurse whose sole responsibility is nursing quality assurance. Instead, the chairperson probably would be a member of the administrative or educational team as well as assuming the role of nursing quality assurance chairperson.

It is recommended that the chairperson hold a department-based nursing leadership position such as the assistant director of nursing, the evening supervisor, a rehabilitation clinical nurse specialist, or a nurse educator. The rationale for department-based instead of unit-based leadership is to minimize the possibilities of bias for or against any one unit. More important, the chairperson needs a departmental perspective when coordinating a quality assurance program.

A departmental perspective implies responsibilities involving the nursing department as a whole instead of unit-specific duties. The evening supervisor, for example, is in a position to observe every unit's nursing performance and the impact of each on the facility's nursing practice in general. Such a global perspective enables the supervisor to coordinate quality assurance activities so that both departmental and unit-specific monitors are established.

Whether formulating the initial committee in a new rehabilitation facility or unit or welcoming new members to an already established one, the chairperson should provide an orientation to the committee's purpose, objectives, and methodology for each member. The nurse managers who appoint committee representatives need this orientation as well so that the most appropriate persons may be selected for membership. An enthusiastic chairperson, committed to promoting the quality assurance process in rehabilitation, will succeed in establishing an efficient committee by involving committee members in all facets of the quality assurance process.

After a thorough orientation, the members should participate in establishing monitors, collecting data, and evaluating results of data collection. If members are able to understand and appreciate the value of nursing quality assurance, they will be able to educate peers and subordinates in the process as well.

But what about the quality assurance needs of the nurses working on a rehabilitation unit within an acute care facility? In these instances the vast majority of nursing concerns are acute care-oriented. The nursing quality assurance chairperson will most likely have an acute care focus, possessing little or no rehabilitation background. Therefore, the nurse manager of the rehabilitation unit must orient the chairperson to the unique needs of a rehabilitation quality assurance program and establish a viable means of communication. A rehabilitation nurse should hold membership on the nursing quality assurance committee. She or he will serve as the chairperson's principal resource for the rehabilitation specialty.

## Clinical Nurse Specialist/Nurse Educator

The role of the rehabilitation clinical nurse specialist and the nursing education (staff development) department in nursing quality assurance is extremely important. If not unit-based, either a clinical nurse specialist or nurse educator may qualify as chairperson. As committee members, their educational expertise may be of great assistance in orienting nurses to the concepts of nursing quality assurance in general and of rehabilitation concerns in particular. In an acute care facility, the nurse responsible for staff development on the rehabilitation unit may be a valuable representative of rehabilitation concerns to the committee. This person may also assist rehabilitation staff nurses to present quality assurance data more effectively from a rehabilitation perspective. Whoever the resource, the chairperson of an acute care nursing quality assurance committee should include a "rehabilitation expert" on the committee.

### Staff Nurse

The foundation of the nursing quality assurance committee is, of course, the staff nurse. She or he will have both the responsibility and the authority to carry out the facets of the quality assurance process as identified by the quality assurance committee and to orient peers and subordinates to their roles in the formal maintenance of quality care. It is an advantage to foster peer education regarding nursing quality assurance. Peer review projects may have a much more positive impact than similar projects conducted by "authority figures."

If licensed practical nurses and health assistants are members of the nursing department, they should also be members of the nursing quality assurance committee. Quality of care is influenced by any person providing services, regardless of educational background or job description. Education and promotion of quality assurance activities at all staff levels enhance understanding and, ultimately, provision of quality nursing practice.

In an acute care facility, the registered nurse representing rehabilitation must assume the responsibility of educating peers and subordinates (and, depending upon the degree of expertise, the nurse manager) to the quality assurance process. She or he must be an assertive representative helping to initiate a quality assurance process that benefits both acute care and rehabilitation.

## COMMITTEE STRUCTURES

Figure 3-1 identifies the departments and committees within the rehabilitation hospital that participate on the hospital quality assurance committee. Nursing, because of its relationship to patients and families, is one of the key components to an active quality assurance committee.

Figure 3-2 illustrates the working relationship of the nursing quality assurance committee as it reports to the hospital quality assurance committee and the medical executive committee. The nursing quality assurance chairperson is the representative to the hospital quality assurance committee. Each unit is represented on the nursing quality assurance committee along with representation from the nursing educational department, if available.

In Figure 3-3 a spinal cord injury unit serves as an example of different nursing levels participating in the quality assurance activities of the nursing department. It

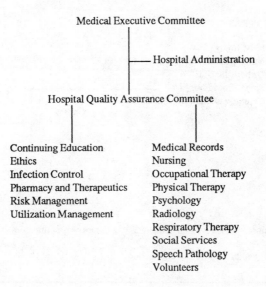

**Figure 3-1** Hospital Quality Assurance

**Figure 3-2** Nursing Quality Assurance Committee Structure

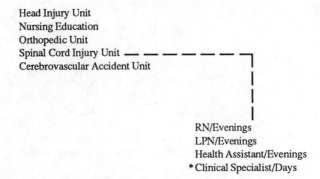

Nursing Quality Assurance Committee:

Head Injury Unit
Nursing Education
Orthopedic Unit
Spinal Cord Injury Unit
Cerebrovascular Accident Unit

RN/Evenings
LPN/Evenings
Health Assistant/Evenings
*Clinical Specialist/Days

\* indicates unit representative to nursing quality assurance committee.

**Figure 3-3**  Unit Quality Assurance Participation

---

is important to include the different levels for reasons previously discussed and to have all shifts represented.

## SUMMARY

Establishing an effective nursing quality assurance committee requires careful selection of members, an organized method of data collection, and an effectively planned format for monitoring. The rehabilitation nurse representing a rehabilitation unit within an acute care facility must be especially well prepared in order to teach acute care colleagues the requirements of rehabilitation nursing quality assurance.

---

### NOTES

1. Christina M. Mumma, ed., *Rehabilitation Nursing: Concepts and Practice—A Core Curriculum*, 2nd ed. (Evanston, Ill.: Rehabilitation Nursing Institute, 1987), 461.

2. Ibid., 462.

3. National Association of Rehabilitation Facilities (NARF) Headquarters, telephone interview, June 1987.

4. Susan Hosek et al., *Charges and Outcomes for Rehabilitative Care—Implications for the Prospective Payment System* (Santa Monica, Calif.: Rand Corporation, 1986), 7.

5. Elizabeth Nancy Lewis and Patricia Vince Carini, *Nurse Staffing and Patient Classification—Strategies for Success* (Rockville, Md.: Aspen Publishers, Inc., 1984), 51.

6. Mumma, *Rehabilitation Nursing*, 460.

7. Ibid.

8. NARF Headquarters, telephone interview, June 1987.

## BIBLIOGRAPHY

Adams, Rella. "The Impact of Utilization Review on Nursing." *Journal of Nursing Administration* 17 (1987): 44-46.

American Nurses' Association. *A Plan for the Implementation of the Standards of Nursing Practice.* Kansas City, Mo.: American Nurses' Association, 1975.

Dai, Yu-Tzu. "Health Beliefs and Compliance with a Skin Care Regimen." *Rehabilitation Nursing* 12 (1987): 13-16.

DeVincezo, Doris K., and Watkins, Sylvia. "Accidental Falls in a Rehabilitation Setting." *Rehabilitation Nursing* 12 (1987): 248-252.

Donabedian, Avedis. *The Definition of Quality and Approaches to Its Assessment.* Ann Arbor, Mich.: Health Administration Press, 1980.

Forguer, Sandra L., and Anderson, Taylor B. "A Concerns-Based Approach to the Implementation of Quality Assurance Systems." *Quality Review Bulletin* 8 (1982): 14-19.

Gallant, Barbara W., and McLane, Audrey M. "Outcome Criteria: A Process for Validation at the Unit Level." *Journal of Nursing Administration* 9 (1979): 14-21.

Hamilton, Sharon. "Implementing a Successful Quality Assurance Program in the Rehabilitation Setting." *Journal of Nursing Quality Assurance* 2 (1987): 49-57.

Harmon, Carol A. "Involving Staff in Nursing Quality Assurance." *Quality Review Bulletin* 6 (1980): 26-30.

Haskin, Joy; Marx, Laurie; and Jesser, Sandra. "How To Start a Nursing QA Program (or Perk Up Your Present One)." *Journal of Nursing Quality Assurance* 2 (Fall 1987): 23.

Hosek, Susan, et al. *Charges and Outcomes for Rehabilitative Care—Implications for the Prospective Payment System.* Santa Monica, Calif: Rand Corporation, 1986.

Howe, Marilyn J. "Developing Instruments for Measurement of Criteria: A Clinical Nursing Practice Perspective." *Nursing Research* 29 (1980): 100-103.

Institute of Medicine. *Assessing Quality in Health Care: An Evaluation.* Washington: National Academy of Sciences, 1976.

Johnston, M.V., and Keith, R.A. "Cost Benefits of Medical Rehabilitation: Review and Critique." *Archives of Physical Medicine and Rehabilitation* 64 (1983): 147-154.

Kelly, C.A. "Quality Circles in the Hospital Setting: Their Current Status and Potential for the Future." *Health Care Management Review* 12 (1987): 55-59.

Krueger, Janelle C. "Establishing Priorities for Evaluation and Evaluation Research: A Nursing Perspective." *Nursing Research* 29, no. 2 (1980): 115-118.

LaMantia, J.G. "A Program Design To Reduce Chronic Readmissions for Pressure Sores." *Rehabilitation Nursing* 12 (1987): 22-25.

Lazerri, Mary B. "Quality Assurance Comes Alive at the Unit Level: QAC's." *Nursing at Stanford* 4 (1982): 1, 12.

Loss, Sandra L., and Goodeve, Samuel, Jr. "Follow-up of Nosocomial Infections on Nursing Units: An Approach to Infection Control." *Quality Review Bulletin* 12 (1986): 243-246.

McClure, Margaret L. "The Long Road to Accountability." *Nursing Outlook* 26 (1978): 47-50.

Moore, Karen R. "Quality Assurance and Nursing Audit: Are They Effective?" *Nursing Management* 13 (1982): 18-22.

O'Brien, Barbara L.; O'Such, Donald J; and Pallette, Susan V. "Setting Realistic Goals for Quality Assurance Monitoring: Patient Falls versus Patient Days." *Quality Review Bulletin* 13 (1987): 339–342.

Oulton, R. "Use of Incident Report Data in a System-Wide Quality Assurance/Risk Management Program." *Quality Review Bulletin* 7 (1981): 2–7.

Phaneuf, Maria C., and Wandelt, Mabel A. "Obstacles to and Potentials for Nursing Quality Appraisal." *Quality Review Bulletin* 7 (1981): 2–5.

Rehabilitation Nursing Institute. *Rehabilitation Nursing Concepts and Practice—A Core Curriculum.* 2nd ed. Evanston, Ill.: Rehabilitation Nursing Institute, 1987.

Riffle, K. "Falls: Kinds, Causes and Prevention." *Geriatric Nursing* 13 (1987): 65–69.

Roberts, Carolyn C. "Quality Assurance and Risk Management in Small and Rural Hospitals: The Roles of Trustees, Administration, and Medical Staff." *Quality Review Bulletin* 13 (1987): 205–208.

Schroeder, Patricia S., and Maibusch, Regina M., eds. *Nursing Quality Assurance—A Unit-Based Approach.* Rockville, Md.: Aspen Publishers, Inc., 1984.

Schroeder, Patricia S.; Maibusch, Regina M.; Anderson, Cheryl A.; and Formella, Nancy Mansheim. "A Unit-Based Approach to Quality Assurance." *Quality Review Bulletin* 8 (1982): 10–12.

Sniff, David. "The Evolution of a Quality Assurance Program." *Quality Review Bulletin* 6 (1980): 26–29.

Swartzbeck, E., and Milligan, W.L. "A Comparative Study of Hospital Incidents." *Nursing Management* 13 (1982): 39–43.

van Maanen, Hanneke M. Th. "Improvement of Quality of Nursing Care: A Goal To Challenge in the Eighties." *Journal of Advanced Nursing* 6 (1981): 3–9.

Young, Delores E., and Ventura, Marlene R. "Application of Nursing Diagnosis in Quality Assessment Research." *Quality Assurance Update* 4 (1980): 1–4.

Zalar, Marianne. "Development of a Unit-Based Nursing Quality Assurance Program." *Nursing at Stanford* 4 (1982): 1, 3, 4.

---

## SUGGESTED READINGS

Adams, Rella. "The Impact of Utilization Review on Nursing." *Journal of Nursing Administration* 17 (1987): 44–46.

Bailet, Howard; Lewis, Judy; Hockheiser, Louis; and Bush, Nancy. "Assessing the Quality of Care." *Nursing Outlook* 23 (1975): 153–159.

Bailey, June T., and Claus, Karen E. *Decision Making in Nursing: Tools for Change.* St. Louis, Mo.: C.V. Mosby Co., 1975.

Benedicter, Helen. *From Nursing Audit to Multidisciplinary Audit.* New York: National League for Nursing, 1977.

Bohnet, Nancy L. "Quality Assurance As an Ongoing Component of Hospice Care." *Quality Review Bulletin* 8, no. 5 (1982): 7–11.

Caldwell, George B. "Use of Employee Surveys in Quality Assurance Programs." *Quality Review Bulletin,* 7, no. 7 (1981): 19–22.

Clifford, J.C. "On the Scene: Beth Israel Hospital." *Nursing Administration Quarterly* 5, no. 3 (1981): 1–5.

Cook, Michael H. "Quality Circles—They Really Work, But . . ." *Training and Development* 36, no. 1 (1982): 4–6.

Daeffler, Reidun JuvKam. "Patient Perceptions of Care Under Team and Primary Nursing." *Journal of Nursing Administration* 5 (1975): 20–26.

Donabedian, Avedis. "Some Issues in Evaluating the Quality of Nursing Care: Part II." *American Journal of Public Health* 59 (1969): 1833–1836.

Downs, Florence S. "Relationship of Findings of Clinical Research and Development of Criteria: A Researcher's Perspective." *Nursing Research* 29 (1980): 94–97.

Eddy, Lyndall, and Westbrook, Linda. "Multidisciplinary Retrospective Patient Care Audit." *American Journal of Nursing* 75 (1975): 961–963.

Fifer, William R. "Quality Assurance: Debate Persists on Goals, Impact, and Methods of Evaluating Care." *Hospitals* 53, no. 7 (1979): 163–167.

Froebe, Doris J., and Bain, R. Joyce. *Quality Assurance Programs and Controls in Nursing.* St. Louis, Mo.: C.V. Mosby Co., 1976.

Gallant, Barbara W., and McLane, Audrey M. "Outcome Criteria: A Process for Validation at the Unit Level." *Journal of Nursing Administration* 9 (1979): 14–21.

Ganong, Joan, and Ganong, Warren. *Help . . . with Nursing Audit: A Management Guide.* Chapel Hill, N.C.: W.L. Ganong, 1975.

Gordon, Marjory. "Determining Study Topics." *Nursing Research* 29 (1980): 83–87.

Harmon, Carol A. "Involving Staff in Nursing Quality Assurance." *Quality Review Bulletin* 6, no. 11 (1980): 26–30.

Hegedus, Kathryn S., and Bourdon, Sharon M. "Evaluation Research: A Quality Assurance Program." *Nursing Administration Quarterly* 5, no. 3 (1981): 26–30.

Hover, Julie, and Zimmer, Marie. "Nursing Quality Assurance: The Wisconsin System." *Nursing Outlook* 26 (1978): 242–248.

Howe, Marilyn. "Establishing Valid and Reliable Criteria: A Clinical Nursing Practice Perspective." *Nursing Research* 29 (1980): 115–118.

Isaac, Stephen, and Michael, William B. *Handbook in Research and Evaluation.* San Diego: EDITS, 1983.

Jenkins, Enid. "Administration—Standards for Care and Their Influence on Nursing." *Australian Nurses' Journal* 11 (1982): 38–40.

Johnson, Arlene. "Communication as the Key to Effective Joint Practice Audit." *Quality Review Bulletin* 2 (1976): 61–65.

Johnson, Jeanne, and Pachano, Audrey. "Planning Patients' Discharge." *Supervisor Nurse* 12 no. 2 (1981): 44–50.

Kahn, Kenneth; Hines, William; Woodson, Arlene; and Burkham-Armstrong, Gabrielle. "A Multidisciplinary Approach to Assessing the Quality of Care in Long Term Care Facilities." *Gerontologist* 17 (1977): 61-65.

Kent, Linda A., and Larson, Elaine. "Evaluating the Effectiveness of Primary Nursing Practice." *Journal of Nursing Administration* 13, no. 1 (1983): 34–41.

Klein, Gerald D. "Implementing Quality Circles: A Hard Look at Some of the Realities." *Personnel* 58, no. 6 (1981): 11–20.

Knudson, Maureen. "Teamwork: The Crux of Multidisciplinary Audit." *Quality Review Bulletin* 2 (1976): 22–23.

Kulpa, Judith, "Interdisciplinary Review in Long Term Care." *Quality Review Bulletin* 4 (1978): 15–21.

Lang, Norma M. "Quality Care—Individual and Collective Responsibility." *American Nurse* 6, no. 9 (1974): 4.

Lang, Norma M. *Quality Assurance in Nursing: A Selected Bibliography.* Washington: Department of Health, Education, and Welfare Publication no. HRA 80–30, 1980.

Lindeman, Carol A. "Measuring Quality of Nursing Care: Part One." *Journal of Nursing Administration* 6, no. 6 (1976): 7–9.

Lindy, Cheryl N. "A Three-Part Approach to Quality Assurance in Nursing." *Quality Review Bulletin* 6 (1980): 12–16.

Mayers, Marlene G; Norby, Ronald B.; and Watson, Annita B. *Quality Assurance for Patient Care: Nursing Perspectives.* New York: Appleton-Century-Crofts, 1977.

McClure, Margaret L. "The Long Road to Accountability." *Nursing Outlook* 26, no. 1 (1978): 47–50.

McLeis, Afaf, and Benner, Patricia. "Process or Product Evaluation." *Nursing Outlook* 23 (1975): 303–307.

Miller, Sister Patricia, and Russel, Dorothy A. "Elements Promoting Satisfaction." *Journal of Gerontological Nursing* 6 (1980): 121–129.

Moores, Brian, and Thompson, Andy. "Getting Feedback." *Health and Social Science Journal* 29 (May 1981): 634–636.

Morrison, Barbara J.; Rehr, Helen; Rosenberg, Gary; and Davis, Samuel. "Consumer Opinion Surveys." *Quality Review Bulletin* 8, no. 2 (1982): 19-24.

National League for Nursing, Department of Baccalaureate and Higher Degree Programs. *Quality Assurance—A Joint Venture.* New York: National League for Nursing, 1975.

Nehring, Virginia, and Geach, Barbara. "Patients' Evaluation of Their Care: Why They Don't Complain." *Nursing Outlook* 21 (1973): 317–321.

*Nursing Quality Assurance Management/Learning System.* Kansas City, Mo.: American Nurses' Association and Sutherland Learning Associates, 1982.

Phaneuf, Maria C. *The Nursing Audit: Profile for Excellence.* New York: Appleton-Century-Crofts, 1972.

Phaneuf, Maria C. "Quality Assurance: A Nursing View." *Hospitals* 47 (1973): 62–68.

Phaneuf, Maria C., and Wandelt, Mabel A. "Obstacles to and Potentials for Nursing Quality Appraisal." *Quality Review Bulletin* 7 (1981): 2–5.

Raymond, David, "Departmental Review: Identification and Analysis of Problems in Diagnostic Radiology." *Quality Review Bulletin* 6, no. 9 (1980): 5–10.

Rinaldi, Leena Aalto, and Rubin, Charlene F. "Adding Retrospective Audit." *American Journal of Nursing* 75 (1975): 256–259.

Routhier, R. Wilda. "Tool for the Evaluation of Patient Care." *Supervisor Nurse* 3 (1972): 15–27.

Ruff, Youna. "Balking at Multidisciplinary Audits." *Hospital Peer Review* 3 (1978): 37.

Sandrick, Karen. "The Whole Is Not Equal to the Sum of Its Parts." *Quality Review Bulletin* 2 (1976): 9–18.

Schaffer, Ken L.; Lindenstein, Joan; and Jennings, Thomas. "Successful QA Program Incorporates New JCAH Standard." *Hospitals* 55, no. 16 (1981): 117–120.

Schmadl, John Charles. "Quality Assurance: Examination of the Concept." *Nursing Outlook* 27 (1979): 462–465.

Sinclair, Carole, and Frankel, Mark. "The Effect of Quality Assurance Activities on the Quality of Mental Health Services." *Quality Review Bulletin* 8, no. 7 (1982): 7–15.

Sniff, David. "The Evolution of a Quality Assurance Program." *Quality Review Bulletin* 6 (1980): 26–29.

Tan, Marva West. "Problem Areas in Multidisciplinary Audit." *Quality Review Bulletin* 4 (1978):

33–35.

Tucker, Edith. "An Alternate Route to Quality Assurance—A Holistic Professionally Autonomous Approach." *Hospital Topics* 59, no. 1 (1981): 22–28.

Vanaguras, Audrone; Egelston, E. Martin; Hopkins, Julie; and Walczak, Regina M. "Principles of Quality Assurance." *Quality Review Bulletin* 5, no. 2 (1979): 3–6.

Waters, Gloria. "Determining Criteria Responsibility." *Hospital Peer Review* 3 (1978): 51.

Woody, Mary F. "An Evaluator's Perspective." *Nursing Research* 29 (1980): 74–77.

Young, Delores E., and Ventura, Marlene R. "Application of Nursing Diagnosis in Quality Assessment Research." *Quality Assurance Update* 4, no. 2 (1980): 1–4.

Zalar, Marianne. "Development of a Unit-Based Nursing Quality Assurance Program." *Nursing at Stanford* 4 (1982): 1, 3, 4.

# Appendix 3-A

# Nursing Quality Assurance Program

## PURPOSE

The department of nursing of _____ Rehabilitation Hospital provides patient care services that are optimal within the available resources and are consistent with the objectives, goals, and mission of the department of nursing and the hospital. The purpose of the nursing quality assurance program is to monitor, evaluate, and improve the quality and appropriateness of patient care through a systematic and ongoing process.

## OBJECTIVES

- to evaluate nursing practice by establishment of monitors and criteria for analysis of patient care based on written standards
- to identify trends, problems, or areas in nursing practice needing improvement
- to monitor the appropriateness, timeliness, and effectiveness of problem resolutions that impact on patient care and nursing practice
- to improve communication and integration of activities with other departments in order to facilitate continuity and consistency in the provision of patient care
- to involve nursing personnel in quality assurance activities

## AUTHORITY/PROGRAM ACCOUNTABILITY

The director of nursing retains final authority for the implementation of nursing quality assurance activities. An appointed nursing quality assurance chairperson is responsible for the coordination of such activities in conjunction with the nursing quality assurance committee. The chairperson is the departmental representative to the hospital quality assurance committee and is responsible for reporting quality assurance activities to the committee, the director of nursing, and the medical executive committee.

The nursing quality assurance committee is responsible for the planning and monitoring of quality assurance activities that evaluate the quality and appropriateness of patient care. The committee participates in the ongoing and systematic problem identification and resolution process. This includes the establishment of priorities for the problems that have an impact on the delivery of appropriate and effective patient care in order to improve the quality of nursing services. The nursing quality assurance committee meets at least monthly and is composed of unit/department-based representatives from each nursing clinical area and all shifts. The nurse manager (or designee) of each clinical unit is responsible for quality assurance activities in that area. Responsibilities of the committee include

- establishment of objective criteria that monitor and evaluate the standards of patient care and the quality and appropriateness of nursing and patient care outcomes
- identification, compilation, and assessment of collected data and preparation of reports provided to the director of nursing, clinical area nurse managers, hospital quality assurance committee, medical executive committee, and others as needed
- assessment of problems identified in patient care and evaluation of action taken to resolve problems and improve care
- annual review of the effectiveness of the monitoring, evaluation, and problem resolution process of the nursing department
- performance of annual review of the nursing quality assurance program
- documentation of minutes of all committee meetings
- integration of nursing quality assurance activities with the interdisciplinary team and the hospital quality assurance program, including program evaluation and joint studies
- development/presentation of quarterly nursing quality assurance summaries to the hospital quality assurance committee
- establishment of subcommittees to monitor and evaluate policies, procedures, and performance standards and standards of care
- facilitation of nursing education to improve patient care
- assurance of confidentiality and proper use of data collected through quality assurance activities (confidentiality policies of _____ Rehabilitation Hospital observed)

## PROGRAM IMPLEMENTATION

### Monitoring and Data Collection

Nursing practice is compared with standards of practice as established by the department of nursing of _____ Rehabilitation Hospital. The development of standards is based on external standards of government, accrediting, and professional organizations (i.e., American Nurses' Association, Association of Rehabilitation Nurses, Joint Commission on Accreditation of Healthcare Organizations, Commission on Accreditation of Rehabilitation Facilities, and licensing standards).

Monitors of structure, process, and outcome standards are established with acceptable levels of practice criteria identified (see Exhibit 3-A-1). Data for each monitor are collected and evaluated, and the results—including action taken—are reported to the nursing quality assurance committee (see Exhibit 3-A-2). Data collection is achieved through prospective, concurrent, and retrospective review as appropriate. Periodic reporting (monthly, quarterly, semiannually, etc.) is recommended at the time the monitor is established and is reviewed/revised as necessary. Those reports demonstrate the rate or percentage occurrence and other information of interest derived from analysis of the findings.

### Problem Identification/Resolutions

Problems are identified through monitoring the following quality assurance activities (not inclusive).

- nursing documentation
- patient satisfaction surveys
- problem identification forms
- adverse occurrence reports
- infection control reports
- patient/family/staff interviews
- program evaluation information/results
- communication from hospital committees
  1. infection control
  2. risk management
  3. quality assurance
  4. utilization management
  5. medical records

**Exhibit 3-A-1** Nursing Quality Assurance Monitors

| Standard | Monitor | Frequency of Data Collection | Expected Outcome Criteria | Method of Retrieval (Person[s] Responsible) |
|----------|---------|------------------------------|---------------------------|---------------------------------------------|
|          |         |                              |                           |                                             |

**Exhibit 3-A-2** Nursing Quality Assurance: Summary Report

| Monitor | Findings | Analysis | Action/Follow Up |
|---|---|---|---|

Month(s)/Year

Check:
_____ Monthly Summary
_____ Quarterly Summary

6. safety committee
7. pharmacy and therapeutics
8. case management
9. administration
10. medical executive committee
11. nurse administration meetings
12. unit staff meetings

- evaluation of patient and staff educational programs
- patient, family, staff complaints/compliments
- medical record reviews
- accreditation surveys
- patient acuity
- hours of nursing care provided
- 24-hour reports from nursing units/supervisors
- performance evaluations
- case conferences

The nursing quality assurance committee participates in the problem identification/resolution process for referral of problems identified from the various sources. In conjunction with the hospital quality assurance committee, the nursing quality assurance committee monitors trends and evaluates information resulting from the problem identification/resolution process. Problems are documented—including action taken, resolution, and evaluation—and are reviewed by the nursing quality assurance committee.

Identified problems are resolved at the lowest level possible. Priority is established for problems that have an impact on the delivery and effectiveness of patient care. In establishing problem priority consider whether the problems

- result in the delay/appropriateness of care
- result from inconsistency in implementation of nursing practice based on standards, policies, procedures, and guidelines as established by the department of nursing
- have an impact on patient outcomes (e.g., program evaluation)
- involve a lengthy resolution
- involve other units, disciplines, or services
- are isolated or recurring
- justify the time, effort, cost, and manpower needed to investigate and resolve them

Problems may be resolved by the following:

- development of educational programs
- changes in existing resources (e.g., staffing patterns, supplies, equipment)
- reallocation of expenditures
- reassessment/revisions of goals, objectives, and standards of the department of nursing
- integration with other interdisciplinary team members
- counseling of personnel, including progressive disciplinary action

The resolution and corrective action should address the cause of the problem. In order to achieve an effective outcome, the plan of action should identify the expected change, who is responsible for effecting the change, the appropriate action (considering the severity and priority of the problem), and the anticipated time of resolution.

The authority for problem resolution in the department of nursing is with nurse managers, the director of nursing, the nursing quality assurance committee, and integration with the hospital quality assurance committee. However, all nursing personnel are responsible for problem identification/resolution. Resolution involves referral through the appropriate channels—unit management, interdisciplinary team members, nursing administration, hospital administration, and the medical executive committee.

## BIBLIOGRAPHY

Hamilton, Sharon. "Implementing a Successful Quality Assurance Program in the Rehabilitation Setting." *Journal of Nursing Quality Assurance* 2, no. 1 (1987): 49–57.

Joint Commission on Accreditation of Healthcare Organizations. *Accreditation Manual for Hospitals.* Chicago: Joint Commission on Accreditation of Healthcare Organizations, 1988.

Joint Commission on Accreditation of Healthcare Oraganizations. *Monitoring and Evaluation of the Quality and Appropriateness of Care.* Chicago: Joint Commission on Accreditation of Healthcare Organizations, 1986.

Marx, Laurie, and Haskin, Joy. "Nursing Q.A.: Step Two, Standards." *Journal of Quality Assurance* 10, no. 1 (1988): 24–25.

*Quality Assurance—A Guide and Workbook for Developing a Quality Assessment/Monitoring Program.* Blackwood, N.J.: Diversified Business Associates, 1987.

# Chapter 4

# Strategies for Program Implementation

## INTRODUCTION

Implementation of the nursing quality assurance program is accomplished through planned, systematic, and ongoing reviews. Focus should be placed on improvement in patient care and problems affecting that care. This process, as identified in Chapter 3, involves monitoring of the quality and appropriateness of nursing care provided via monitoring of the department's nursing standards of care. These standards are established from rehabilitation nursing standards and standards of the American Nurses' Association, the Joint Commission on Accreditation of Healthcare Organizations, and the Commission on Accreditation of Rehabilitation Facilities. In addition, in rehabilitation nursing, nursing quality assurance must integrate the nursing unit(s) and departmental activities into program evaluation and hospital quality assurance. Nursing quality assurance envelops not just nursing, but it must have direction and involvement with the other disciplines in the hospital. The commitment and involvement of all levels of the nursing staff are the basis for a successful program.

Some of the issues pertinent to nursing rehabilitation, as identified in Chapter 3, are explored further here, focusing on setting up the monitor, collecting the data (including sample forms used in data collection), and reporting the data to the nursing quality assurance committee for analysis, evaluation, and appropriate action.

## MONITORING

### Falls

Patient falls may be monitored with the cooperation of the hospital's risk management office, the nursing units, nursing quality assurance, and other disciplines (e.g., physical therapy, occupational therapy, therapeutic recreation). On an ongoing basis, usually monthly, statistics are forwarded to the nursing quality assurance committee. This does not mean that individual falls are not looked into immediately. Each patient fall must be reviewed by the nurse manager of the involved unit in order to ensure that preventative measures are instituted. Also, if it is noted by the nurse manager or risk management representative that several falls in the period of one week involved one particular patient, action is taken at the time of the occurrence, not waiting until monthly statistics have been completed. Exhibit 4-1 is an example of monitors of patient falls by nursing quality assurance. From previous experience, these areas (falls occurring in-hospital and during therapeutic home visits) were determined to be significant to the patient's health and safety as well as potential hospital liabilities. The "finder" is the hospital staff member reporting the fall.

*Fall Prevention Program*

A fall prevention program may become an important part of the nursing quality assurance program. Such a program can be designed to identify patients with an increased risk for falls before they are admitted to the rehabilitation facility/unit, whenever possible. Patients who are admitted without a known history of falls may be placed on the program also.

Prior to admission, a liaison nurse may visit a potential rehabilitation patient while in acute care. The communication of a patient's fall history is important in setting up a plan of care upon the patient's admission. The liaison nurse informs a risk management representative and the nurse manager of the impending admission and fall history. The team is informed, and planning for safe care begins. If a liaison nurse does not see all patients, another communication system can be implemented. Upon referral for admission, the information is asked of the social worker, primary nurse, physician, or therapist of the referring hospital and communicated to the nurse manager of the accepting unit. Whatever the method, the importance is that the team is aware of the problem.

If the patient does not have a known history of falls upon admission, the patient's medical condition, age, medications, and behavioral and debilitating factors are evaluated. A patient may be placed on the fall prevention program at that time. If a patient falls while in rehabilitation, the patient's fall is evaluated by the risk management representative, nurse manager, and the team to determine whether the patient is at continued risk for falls or whether the occurrence was a single event.

Because of the physical and/or cognitive deficits affecting most rehabilitation patients, these patients are at an increased risk for falls. However, for example,

**Exhibit 4-1** Nursing Quality Assurance Monitors

| Standard | Monitor | Frequency of Data Collection | Expected Outcome Criteria | Method of Retrieval (Person[s] Responsible) |
|---|---|---|---|---|
| Safe patient care will be provided through fall prevention techniques | No. of patient falls (in-hospital) reported | Monthly | Goal: 0 occurrences Accept: Less than 12 occurrences | Adverse occurrence reports (finder to Risk Management) |
| | No. of patient falls on therapeutic home visits | Monthly | Goal: 0 occurrences Accept: Less than 3 occurrences | Adverse occurrence reports (finder to Risk Management) |

just because the elderly patient in general has been identified to be at risk does not mean that placement on a structured fall prevention program is necessary. A more individualized evaluation determines whether that elderly patient is alert and oriented, has good balance and good judgment, and is safe for ambulation independently or safe for wheelchair or walker independence. It may not be necessary for such a patient to be in the fall prevention program. This does not mean that safety precautions are not taken with all patients. It is a goal of a rehabilitation program that patients achieve a maximal level of functioning. Allowing the patient independence is imperative to meeting this goal.

An example of a patient requiring placement on a fall prevention program is a 19-year-old motorcycle accident victim who sustained a closed head injury with resulting cognitive deficits. Upon visitation in the acute care setting, the rehabilitation liaison nurse was informed about the patient's impulsiveness. The patient had fallen once "even though he was restrained in bed." The patient's fall and documentation of his impulsive behavior were reported to the nurse manager at the rehabilitation hospital where the patient was to be transferred. As a result, upon admission to the unit, the patient was placed on a fall prevention program. The nursing and team plan of care addressed the patient's need for one-to-one supervision to eliminate the need for restraints, which increased the patient's agitation and confusion. In addition, the patient was closely monitored for persons and situations that increased his impulsive behavior.

A fall prevention program involves communication to the case manager and the interdisciplinary team, identification of the problem and inclusions into the patient's plan of care, and evaluation of the patient's abilities as progress is made toward independence. A sticker indicating that the patient is on a fall prevention program can be placed on the patient's chart and sometimes on the patient's wheelchair. All hospital staff, the patient, and family members are alerted to the meaning of the sticker. Since the patient may be alert and oriented and may not need constant supervision, having progressed to allowing off-unit wheelchair mobility on even and uneven surfaces, the fall prevention sticker serves to alert staff members not familiar with the patient to unsafe situations witnessed.

Evaluating a fall prevention program by reviewing patients identified at risk and comparing them with the actual number of falls that they may experience may be helpful in assisting nursing and other disciplines in the planning and education needed to decrease fall occurrences. Continuing education of patients, family members, and staff is vital in the success of a fall prevention program. Not every fall will be prevented, but the heightened awareness to safety that a fall prevention program accomplishes can decrease the chance of a fall occurring.

A format for reporting the statistics regarding in-hospital patient falls on a cerebrovascular accident unit is displayed in Table 4-1. These collected data from risk management will be analyzed further by the nurse manager and the nursing quality assurance committee.

**Table 4-1** Format for Reporting Patient Falls on a 30-Bed Cerebrovascular Accident Unit (Reporting period: June 1988)

| Patient | Age/Sex | Fall Location | How Occurred | A/U* | Time | LOS* (days) | On FPP* |
|---|---|---|---|---|---|---|---|
| 1 | 39/F | Bedside | Transferring from wheelchair to bed | U | 8:40 P.M. | 21 | No |
| 2 | 72/M | Bedside | Climbing out of bed | U | 12:05 A.M. | 9 | Yes |
| 3 | 81/M | Bedside | Reaching from wheelchair for glasses | U | 6:50 A.M. | 45 | No |
| 4 | 53/M | PT gym | Ambulating with quad cane | A | 10:00 A.M. | 43 | Yes |
| 5 | 48/M | Bathroom | Lost balance, knee buckled | A | 7:20 P.M. | 16 | Yes |
| 6 | 67/F | Unit dining room | Ambulating with walker | U | 4:45 P.M. | 38 | No |

*A, attended by staff; U, unattended by staff; LOS, length of stay at time of fall; FPP, fall prevention program.

## Patient Satisfaction Questionnaire

The satisfaction or complaints that a patient expresses are helpful in planning and improving patient care. A patient satisfaction questionnaire is one of the ways for a rehabilitation unit or facility to measure successful patient outcomes. Used alone, the patient satisfaction questionnaire is not sufficient in evaluating the rehabilitation program, but when used in conjunction with other measurement tools (e.g., independence gain measurement, education evaluation, discharge follow-up) can give the team an indication of the program's success and areas needing improvement.

There are several benefits in collecting information from patient satisfaction questionnaires. Not asking patients how they feel about the care they received and not responding to their dislikes "results in patients' talking about their terrible care to everyone else."[1] A dissatisfied patient can have great influence on a contact they may have who may use the facility in the future. The patient will be more satisfied if allowed to express feelings regarding the care received. This input assists the hospital and the team in making decisions about care and the way they are perceived.

Determining the type of questionnaire and questions to be asked requires input from the team. A patient satisfaction questionnaire is a monitor of the quality and appropriateness of care received from the patient's view. Consideration should be given as to what questions would best reflect the outcome of the program. A pilot test of the developed questionnaire assists in rating its validity. Is a questionnaire wanted that addresses the overall rehabilitation program, or one that is more specific to a certain group of patients or unit (e.g., spinal cord-injured patients, head-injured patients, or stroke patients)? Is a questionnaire desired that is discipline-specific or that involves all disciplines? Exhibit 4-2 identifies sample questions on a more generic rehabilitation questionnaire. Exhibit 4-3 is a sample questionnaire used by nursing on a stroke rehabilitation unit. Questions should be formulated with the patient population in mind. They should be easy to understand and to answer, requiring check boxes, short answers, or circling the appropriate answer, and not be time-consuming. This will encourage participation.

Another consideration is deciding how the data will be collected. Data can be collected in person, by telephone, or by a written questionnaire. Collecting data in person has the benefit of being more personal and allowing an explanation of the questions and responses but can be embarrassing to the interviewee and interviewer, thus possibly blocking honest answers. This method requires specially trained interviewers to ease this problem and is also time-consuming. Telephone questionnaires are also personal, allow a more detailed explanation of the patient's feelings and concerns, and give distance and a feeling of nonidentity to lessen embarrassment. However, the telephone interview is often viewed as a nuisance to the interviewee. The telephone method is also time-consuming and not as cost-effective. The written questionnaire has the disadvantage of being impersonal but the advantage of encouraging the patient to be honest, as long as confidentiality is assured. This method is more cost-effective, taking the least staff time for data collection, and is not very expensive to develop or implement.

It will also need to be decided who will collect the data: the patient or family member, a known caregiver, or an unknown staff member. Not all patients will be able to complete a written questionnaire or participate in a telephone survey. If a discharge telephone survey/questionnaire is used, it is helpful to coordinate calling with other team members in order to limit the number of similar calls to a patient or family. In this circumstance, a coordinated interdisciplinary questionnaire is better than several discipline-specific questionnaires. Nursing would need to include pertinent questions to evaluate expected outcomes.

When should the patient satisfaction questionnaire be implemented? The telephone survey/questionnaire will need to be performed after the patient's discharge, probably within the first one to two weeks. This can be coordinated with the follow-up telephone call from nursing, if that is used at the facility. A personal interview/questionnaire could be done toward the end of the patient's stay. The patient may receive the written questionnaire at discharge from the primary nurse, case manager, social worker, or other designated staff member. An explanation on completing the form and instruction to drop off or mail back (stamped

**Exhibit 4-2** Sample Questions for a Patient Satisfaction Questionnaire

---

1. Who recommended this rehabilitation program to you?

    _____ Doctor

    _____ Nurse or therapist

    _____ Family member

    _____ Friend

    _____ Other (please specify) _____

2. Were you visited by a nurse from this hospital before you were admitted here?

    _____ Yes

    _____ No

    If so, was the program explained to you?

    _____ Yes

    _____ No

    Were you given a patient information booklet?

    _____ Yes

    _____ No

3. Were you involved in the planning of your care?

    _____ Yes

    _____ No

4. Was your family involved in the planning of your care?

    _____ Yes

    _____ No

5. Was the staff helpful in meeting your needs?

    _____ Yes

    _____ No

6. Were your questions about your care answered?

    _____ Yes

    _____ No

7. Were you taught about your medications?

    _____ Yes

    _____ No

8. Did you attend a support group while in the hospital?

    _____ Yes

    _____ No

    Was it helpful?

    _____ Yes

    _____ No

    Did your family attend a support group?

    _____ Yes

    _____ No

    Was it helpful?

    _____ Yes

    _____ No

**Exhibit 4-2** continued

9. Please rate the following services (place an X in the appropriate box):

| | Poor | Fair | Good | Excellent |
|---|---|---|---|---|
| Dietary | | | | |
| Doctors | | | | |
| Nursing | | | | |
| Occupational therapy | | | | |
| Physical therapy | | | | |
| Psychology | | | | |
| Therapeutic recreation | | | | |
| Social work | | | | |
| Speech | | | | |

10. Did you go on a therapeutic home visit while here?

    \_\_\_\_ Yes

    \_\_\_\_ No

Were you prepared for the visit?

    \_\_\_\_ Yes

    \_\_\_\_ No

Comments: _____

_____

11. Did you learn what you expected to learn while you were here?

    \_\_\_\_ Yes

    \_\_\_\_ No

Comments: _____

_____

12. Do you feel ready to leave the hospital?

    \_\_\_\_ Yes

    \_\_\_\_ No

13. How satisfied were you with the care you received?

    \_\_\_\_ Very satisfied

    \_\_\_\_ Satisfied

    \_\_\_\_ Dissatisfied

    \_\_\_\_ Very dissatisfied

14. Would you recommend the hospital to others?

    \_\_\_\_ Yes

    \_\_\_\_ No

15. What did you like *most* about the hospital? _____

_____

16. What did you like *least* about the hospital? _____

_____

17. Additional comments _____

_____

18. Who is completing this questionnaire?

    \_\_\_\_ Patient

    \_\_\_\_ Family member

    \_\_\_\_ Friend

**Exhibit 4-3** Sample Stroke Unit Patient Satisfaction Questionnaire

_____ Rehabilitation Hospital
Patient Satisfaction Questionnaire: Stroke Unit

We value our patients' opinions. Please respond to these questions so that we can evaluate and improve our services. This can be completed by your family member or a friend if you choose.

1. Who welcomed you to the unit upon your arrival?
   _____ Your primary nurse
   _____ Your case manager
   _____ Your doctor
   _____ Secretary
   _____ Other
   _____ Don't know

2. What is the name of your primary nurse?
   _____

3. What is the name of your case manager?
   _____

4. Do you feel that your privacy was respected by the nurses?
   _____ Yes
   _____ No
   Comments: _____

5. Were you involved in planning your care?
   _____ Yes
   _____ No
   Comments: _____

6. Was your family involved in planning your care?
   _____ Yes
   _____ No
   Comments: _____

7. Did you attend the stroke education classes?
   _____ Yes
   _____ No
   Were they helpful?
   _____ Yes
   _____ No
   Comments: _____

**Exhibit 4-3** continued

8. Do you feel that you improved while you were here?
    _____ Yes
    _____ No
    Comments: _____
    _____

9. Do you feel ready to be discharged?
    _____ Yes
    _____ No
    Comments: _____
    _____

10. Would you recommend this unit to others needing this type of service?
    _____ Yes
    _____ No
    Comments: _____
    _____

11. What did you like *least* about the nursing care you received? _____
    _____

12. What did you like *most* about the nursing care you received? _____
    _____
    _____

13. Who completed this questionnaire?
    _____ Patient
    _____ Family member
    _____ Friend

14. If you would like to talk with an administrative representative about your care or any concerns you may have, please sign your name below and leave a phone number where you may be reached or you may call an administrative representative at extension
    _____ .
    Name _____
    Phone Number _____

Thank you for responding to this questionnaire. Please place it in the envelope attached and return it in the box marked "Patient Satisfaction Questionnaire" in the lobby.

envelope provided) could be given at this time. Written instructions as to what to do with the completed form and who can complete the form should be included on the questionnaire.

The patient's successful outcome is a measurement not only of functional gains but of feelings about his or her care and progress. As stated, the patient satisfaction questionnaire can be an effective quality assurance monitor. Nurses can utilize the information from data collected to revise programs, plan patient and staff education, and evaluate their own performance.

## Nosocomial Infections

The importance of monitoring nosocomial infections in the rehabilitation setting is as important as in any other hospital. In addition to the effects on the patient's condition, hospital-acquired infections can add significantly to the patient's length of stay. This obviously affects the cost of the hospitalization.

It is often difficult to determine a nosocomial infection in rehabilitation because of the structure of the environment and the patient's program. Rehabilitation patients may be involved in community outings or activities on another unit as part of their program. The patients will probably participate in therapeutic home visits with their families in preparation for discharge. The patients and/or the families will participate in the provision of care (e.g., intermittent catheterization program, tracheostomy care, or wound care).

Evaluation of data from infection control will assist in identifying trends and patterns in types of infections and their location, in determining the effectiveness of treatment, and in isolating the mode of transmission. This information assists nursing in developing or refining educational programs for patients, their families, and staff, and in evaluating nursing practice. Table 4-2 shows an example of data that may be reported by infection control to the unit nurse manager and the nursing quality assurance committee on a monthly basis. The data conveyed are helpful only in relationship to the knowledge of "averages," exceptional circumstances, and data from the previous month(s). Some variables to consider when evaluating data are patient census, patient acuity, therapeutic home visits, new procedures, and how the specimen was collected.

Table 4-2 shows that there were more total infections on the spinal cord injury unit, most of which were urinary tract infections (UTIs). Closer inspection determined that, of the six patients with UTIs, five had undergone intermittent

**Table 4-2** Monthly Nosocomial Infection Report from Infection Control to Nursing Quality Assurance (June 1988)

| Unit* | Type of Infection | | | | |
| --- | --- | --- | --- | --- | --- |
| | Wound | Urinary Tract | Respiratory | Systemic | Total |
| Spinal cord injury | 1 | 6 | 1 | 0 | 8 |
| Head injury | 0 | 1 | 2 | 0 | 3 |
| Stroke | 0 | 3 | 1 | 1 | 5 |
| Orthopedic | 3 | 0 | 0 | 0 | 3 |
| Total | 4 | 10 | 4 | 1 | 19 |

*All units have 30 beds.

catheterizations performed by the nursing staff (see Table 4-3). The nurse manager and infection control nurse may want to investigate further the two patients in the same room with *Escherichia coli* UTIs and other common factors that may exist (for example, same caregivers or equipment similarities). Further staff education or reinforcement of standards of care may be needed. In some instances, as with patient 2, the patient may need further observation and instruction in performing the intermittent self-catheterization program.

As with fall monitoring, it is not necessary or advisable to wait until monthly statistics are presented before action is implemented. Information from infection control should be made available to nursing in order to protect the patients and staff from nosocomial infections. The nosocomial infection rate is one of the more important indicators of quality and appropriate nursing practice.

## Peer Review

Nursing quality assurance has traditionally looked at peer review in measuring actual performance to the standards of care identified by the department. The present focus is toward monitoring the quality and appropriateness of nursing care and its impact on patient outcomes.[2] Rehabilitation nursing is patient-outcome-oriented, establishing goals with the patient and family and working toward those goals. Therefore, monitors that measure the appropriateness of the care provided should be implemented.

Considerations of the peer review process include the following:

- Confidentiality of findings must be maintained. Much concern surrounding peer review is the availability of information. This refers to confidentiality of the practitioner as well as the patient information that is revealed. Practice measures need to be built into the review process.
- Reports of findings (summary) should be shared with the staff, the unit, and departmental quality assurance.
- The main purpose of peer review, as with any monitoring tool, is to evaluate the appropriateness of care; change should be effected when indicated to improve nursing care.

Nursing peer review takes many forms. Emphasis may be placed on monitoring documentation, evaluation of education, competency skills (e.g., starting IVs, performing catheterizations), or management skills. Effective peer review must utilize objective criteria, be easy to use, be tested for validity, and be reliable. Methods of review best used are concurrent (i.e., direct observation of care given or timeliness of documentation reviews) and retrospective chart reviews.

The performance of nursing peer review can be a function of the nursing quality assurance coordinator, unit nurse manager, and/or members of the nursing quality

**Table 4-3** Nosocomial Urinary Tract Infections on 30-Bed Spinal Cord Injury Unit (June 1988)

| Patient | Room # | ICP* | ICP Performed by | Type of Specimen | Organism | Date of Admission | Onset Date |
|---------|--------|------|------------------|------------------|----------|-------------------|------------|
| 1 | 106 | Yes | Nursing staff | Catheter | *Escherichia coli* | 5/15/88 | 6/3/88 |
| 2 | 121 | Yes | Patient | Catheter | *Escherichia coli* | 6/1/88 | 6/18/88 |
| 3 | 102 | Yes | Nursing staff | Catheter | *Staphylococcus aureus* | 6/11/88 | 6/22/88 |
| 4. | 110 | Yes | Nursing staff | Catheter | *Pseudomonas aeruginosa* | 5/24/88 | 6/5/88 |
| 5 | 106 | Yes | Nursing staff | Catheter | *Escherichia coli* | 6/2/88 | 6/10/88 |
| 6 | 118 | Yes | Nursing staff | Catheter | *Klebsiella pneumoniae* | 5/23/88 | 6/28/88 |

*ICP, intermittent catheterization program.

assurance committee. This eases some of the pressure that peer review can cause. Judgment should be placed on the appropriateness of care instead of on any individual practitioner.

Implementation of QA that involves a peer review approach may require consistent education and encouragement of staff members regarding the issues of professionalism and accountability[3]

The benefits of nursing peer review include

- heightened awareness of nursing care being provided
- increased understanding of nursing practice standards and appropriateness of care

**Exhibit 4-4** Evaluation of Documentation on Multidisciplinary Care Plan

---

1. Patient's name _____
2. Patient's ID # _____
3. Diagnosis _____
4. Unit _____

MONITORING CRITERIA

5. Was the care plan initiatied within 3–5 days of the patient's admission?
   - _____ Yes
   - _____ No

6. Were initial evaluation assessments documented within 48 hours of admission?

| | Yes | No | Not Ordered |
|---|---|---|---|
| Dietary | _____ | _____ | _____ |
| Medical | _____ | _____ | _____ |
| Nursing | _____ | _____ | _____ |
| Occupational therapy | _____ | _____ | _____ |
| Physical therapy | _____ | _____ | _____ |
| Therapeutic recreation | _____ | _____ | _____ |
| Social work | _____ | _____ | _____ |

7. Were the patient's goals documented?
   - _____ Yes
   - _____ No

8. Were problems in care identified?
   - _____ Yes
   - _____ No

- increased ability of staff in review practice
- positive feedback to staff in accomplishments and participation in decisions to revise practice

Exhibits 4-4, 4-5, and 4-6 represent samples of monitoring activities used in nursing peer review.

## Medication Variations

Monitoring variations in the administration of patients' medications is a concern of nursing professionals. The nursing quality assurance committee in rehabilitation will want to review medication variations routinely, as they may be the result of poor nursing care and lead to costly repercussions for the patient, the hospital, and the nurse.

Rehabilitation nurses are responsible for making sure that the patient has been instructed in the administration of medications and demonstrates understanding by return demonstration. Not only do the patients have a right to know about the medications they are taking, but it is imperative that they have this knowledge in progressing toward and achieving independence. The emphasis on consistent teaching involvement with the patient can indeed lead to a low rate of medication variations.

Medication variations are reviewed by looking at rate of occurrence per unit and for the facility, multiple occurrences with one patient or by one nurse, and other variables such as

- wrong medication given or taken
- wrong time of administration
- wrong dosage given or taken
- omitted medication
- place of occurrence (in-hospital or during therapeutic home visit)
- effects on patient
- follow-up care needed, if any

A problem that may surface in rehabilitation is the patient's compliance to the medication schedule while on therapeutic home visits (THV). This can be too much, too little, not taking the medication at all, or taking the medication in conjunction with noncompatible substances (e.g., food, alcohol, other medications). In a sample rehabilitation facility, before a patient is released for a THV, the patient must be able to administer his or her medications safely. Since admission to the hospital, the nursing staff has worked with the patient and family

**Exhibit 4-5** Peer Review: Therapeutic Home Visit (THV) Documentation

---

THV Documentation Evaluation

Patient ID #_____    THV date _____
Unit _____

Prior to the patient's THV, was the following documented in the progress notes?
1. Time patient left
   _____ Yes
   _____ No
2. How patient left (ambulatory, wheelchair, crutches, etc.)
   _____ Yes
   _____ No
3. Who accompanied the patient
   _____ Yes
   _____ No
4. Any medications sent with patient
   _____ Yes
   _____ No
5. Any care needs sent with patient
   _____ Yes
   _____ No
6. Instructions to patient and/or family
   _____ Yes
   _____ No
7. Release signed
   _____ Yes
   _____ No

Upon the patient's return from the THV was the following documented in the progress notes?
8. Time patient returned
   _____ Yes
   _____ No
9. How patient returned
   _____ Yes
   _____ No
10. Who accompanied the patient
   _____ Yes
   _____ No
11. Medications returned not given
   _____ Yes
   _____ No
12. Problems reported
   _____ Yes
   _____ No

Chart reviewed by _____    Date reviewed _____
Upon completion, please forward to the Nursing QA Coordinator

---

**Exhibit 4-6** Timeliness of Follow-up Phone Calls: Quarterly Evaluation

Criterion 1:  Follow-up phone calls will be made by the patient's primary nurse within 7–14 days of the patient's discharge.

Criterion 2:  Documentation on the "Follow-up Discharge Call" form will be complete.

| PATIENT ID # | DISCHARGE DATE | DATE OF CALL | WAS FORM COMPLETED? | PRIMARY NURSE |
|---|---|---|---|---|
| 1. | | | | |
| 2. | | | | |
| 3. | | | | |
| 4. | | | | |
| 5. | | | | |
| 6. | | | | |
| 7. | | | | |
| 8. | | | | |
| 9. | | | | |
| 10. | | | | |

This review is to be completed on each primary nurse by each unit's nurse manager on a quarterly basis. Summary data only are to be forwarded to the Nursing QA Coordinator.

Nurse manager _____
Review data _____

using medication instruction cards, medication identification charts, and return demonstration methods. The established goal was for the patient to be able to identify the medication, know why it was taken, know the dosage and frequency of administration, name the possible side effects, know where the drug should be kept, know what to do if dosage was missed, and know the drug's incompatibilities with other medications, foods, and alcohol.

In Table 4-4, the medication variations for a 30-bed head injury unit were viewed by the unit quality assurance coordinator. None of the patients required major medical intervention. There were no obvious patterns/trends. The quality assurance coordinator would note the variations by the two nurses for reference to previous variations. Any corrective action would be taken by the nurse manager. Data reported to the hospital quality assurance committee do not make reference to specific nurse involvement. It is important to keep such information confidential for protection of the parties involved and to encourage honest reporting when

**Table 4-4**    Medication Variations on a 30-Bed Head Injury Unit: Nursing Quality Assurance Medication Variation Report (March 1988)

| Patient | Where Occurred | Administered by | Time | Type of Variation | Medical Intervention |
|---------|----------------|-----------------|------|-------------------|----------------------|
| 1 | Unit | Nurse 062 | 6:30 A.M. | Omission | Schedule change |
| 2 | THV | Patient | 8:00 P.M. | Omission | None |
| 3 | Unit | Patient | 8:30 A.M. | Omission | None |
| 4 | Unit | Nurse 024 | 4:00 P.M. | Wrong time | None |

variations occur. All medication variations are reviewed independently for inappropriateness of care and appropriateness of follow up. The patient who omitted a medication while on THV "just forgot" and did not know whether or not to take two at the next due time. This information was conveyed to the nurse upon the patient's return. Reinforcement of medication instruction began immediately. Action does not wait until the monthly report, but appropriateness of the action taken is reviewed by nursing quality assurance. The nursing quality assurance committee may want to focus on medication variations occurring on THV because it may identify weaknesses in the individual patient's program (for example, the patient's level of independence and compliance) or in the nursing program of care (such as medication instruction).

**Program Evaluation**

What is termed as program evaluation in rehabilitation is the evaluation of the patient's outcome based on the patient's diagnosis and disability and the standards of care established. Each patient's care is reviewed at a team conference, usually held every two weeks. The team reviews the goals established, the progress that the patient is making toward these goals, the care that the patient is receiving, the setting of new goals with the patient, and discharge planning. The team, including nursing, evaluates the quality and appropriateness of patient care. The team should consider the following in meeting their goals.

- a process for the identification and resolution of problems that affect the services provided to the patient
- accountability for the care of the patient
- identification of monitors to evaluate patient outcome
- involvement of the patient and family in the outlined program

The purpose of program evaluation in rehabilitation is synonymous with that of quality assurance: to provide quality and appropriate care to the patient as progression is made toward maximal independent functioning.

The team may want to evaluate the following examples for appropriateness of care provided and effective patient outcomes.

- interdisciplinary educational presentations (e.g., sexuality, coping mechanisms, pain management, understanding stroke deficits)
- measurements of independence gains
- behavioral modification programs
- case management system
- team conference documentation
- identification/documentation of goals in the medical record
- fall occurrences
- unscheduled patient transfers to acute care

When the team analyzes program evaluation data or when problems in program implementation occur, it is important to have equal representation from the disciplines, to have members who are oriented to departmental and team quality assurance and want to participate, and to have an agenda and adequate time for a group meeting. This enables the team to focus on the goal of improving patient care. The monitoring of care is best performed by the providers of that care.

Nursing, as with the other disciplines, cannot be exclusively set apart in program evaluation. All team members share in the success or failure of the program. The team, working together with the patient and family, is the major component of a successful rehabilitation program.

## Problem Identification

A problem is a deviation from the expected outcome that cannot be justified as appropriate under the given circumstances. The monitoring process of quality assurance is designed to identify the presence or absence of problems relating to patient care with the goal of problem resolution and improvement in patient care. Nursing quality assurance must have a mechanism for problem identification and resolution.

Problems in rehabilitation nursing may be identified in the processes of program evaluation, utilization review, case reviews, interdepartmentally and intradepartmentally. The review of adverse patient occurrences via generic screening or an incident-reporting process is one method of problem identification. Hospital quality assurance may have a process, including a documentation form, for identifying problems also. The key to the success of any such process is appropriate reporting. Appropriate reporting calls for involvement of the staff and professional communication techniques. A problem identification process must not be used as a tool of finger pointing or revenge. Nursing may utilize the hospital process if one exists. If not, developing its own is beneficial to the evaluation of the care that is delivered.

The type of form used is not as important as the documentation of the problem through resolution. The information on the problem identification form should

- note the date the problem was reported
- describe the problem, referring to the standard involved when possible
- denote immediate action taken
- state whether the problem was an isolated incident or a recurring problem
- indicate an anticipated time frame for resolution
- indicate the supervisor's knowledge of the problem
- indicate notification of any other unit or department involved
- indicate the plan of action to resolve the problem
- indicate the resolution of the problem and the date of resolution

Problems should be resolved at the lowest level possible (i.e., within the department or between departments). Problems that have arisen in nursing practice are reported to the nursing quality assurance committee (they may already have been resolved) for discussion and possible resolution. Sharing problems helps other units that may be having the same problems, and the benefit of group involvement in the problem-solving process is gained. Unresolved problems are communicated to the resource that may assist in finding a solution—hospital quality assurance. All interdisciplinary committees, departments, and other hospital personnel are responsible for the identification of problems affecting the care and outcome of patients.

Certain effects should be considered in the process of problem identification and resolution.

- how the problem impacts on the efficiency of care
- how the problem impacts on the effectiveness of patient care and outcomes
- how often the problem has occurred, or how many patients are affected or potentially affected
- how long the problem has endured
- how much the resolution will cost
- how many services, departments, or units are involved
- how much time and effort will go into the resolution
- how determined is the staff to solve the problem

Problem identification can result from any of the monitors that are identified in this chapter. One of the functions of a nursing quality assurance committee is to identify strengths and areas needing improvement in patient care and nursing practice. The end goal of improvement in patient care is achieved through communication, dedication, and caring.

## DATA COLLECTION

The nursing quality assurance committee determines the frequency of data collection based on the importance of the activity being monitored and its propensity for widespread effects. The committee must consider such issues as the impact on the effectiveness of patient care and outcomes; the impact on efficiency of care; confidentiality; the number of patients, units, programs, or services affected; the impact on cost-containment efforts; and the motivation of the staff to monitor, evaluate, and correct identified problems. Nursing quality assurance should have a positive impact on nursing practice and patient outcomes. Corrective actions may lead to changes that have a positive or negative effect on patient care.

- policy/procedure revisions or development
- staffing patterns
- accountability
- Educational programs for staff development and patient/family programs

Confidentiality in data collection is a controversial subject. Concern must be given to the privacy of patient information, staff information (peer review data), and the storage of that information. Linda Maciorowski recommends three protective measures for nursing quality assurance programs.

1. combining aspects of nursing research and activities
2. establishing patient permission for various quality assurance activities
3. assessing proposed evaluation study plans for ethical and privacy concerns[4]

It is felt that these measures would advise the patient of the quality assurance activities, giving the patient the right to refuse participation.

Unit and departmental nursing quality assurance must determine the following:

1. Who will collect the data for all or each monitor identified? Data may be collected by the unit, by the department, or through the hospital quality assurance program (including risk management, utilization management,

and infection control).
2. What method of data collection will be used (concurrent or retrospective)?
3. How appropriate is the monitor?
4. How often will data be collected?
5. What is the expected/acceptable outcome?

Once the areas of focus have been determined, the exact method of monitoring and data collection can begin (see Chapter 3).

The purpose of monitoring is to identify and correct problems that greatly affect patient care with the intent to improve patient care. The duration of the monitor and data collection depends on the need for improvement, the liability of no action, and other factors. Data collection and monitoring are continued until the problem is corrected or cannot be solved. Evaluation of the monitors at least annually is recommended. Monitors identify when deviations in nursing practice and patient care occur by comparison to determined levels of expected outcome. Examples would be a noted increase in the number of inappropriate admissions, an increase in the nosocomial infection rate, or evidence of incomplete documentation. Single events, patterns, or trends identified through monitoring are evaluated by the nursing quality assurance committee with action initiated toward successful resolution. The evaluation/action process is addressed in Chapter 5.

### Computerization

Computers alone cannot solve problems, but they are beneficial in handling the volume of data that hospitals today are expected to manage. Advances are being made in user ease and packaged programs available for quality assurance. Whether in the accounting department or in the laboratory, most hospitals are using either packaged or hospital-developed programs in some area.

Nursing certainly has a place for computers as the "increasing accountability and responsibility in professional nursing today requires the nurse to handle more information than ever before."[5] Nursing quality assurance can utilize computers in trending data from monitor review, in developing care plans, in developing and evaluating patient education programs, and in rehabilitation program evaluation, to name only a few. Computer data retrieval is faster than by manual means. Comparing data with those from the previous month or year and reviewing infection data from the patient's entire length of stay are much simpler with the use of a computer. One of the most exciting possibilities is a program for comparing actual patient outcomes to nursing standards of care. With the assistance of computerization, these goals can be achieved.

## REPORTING

Through monitoring reports, nursing quality assurance activities are communicated to the nursing quality assurance committee, nursing administration, the hospital quality assurance committee, and the appropriate hospital management (i.e., administration, medical executive committee, and the board of directors). It is necessary for quality assurance activities to be documented, including the process used, actions taken, and the resulting outcome. Data relating to identified monitors are collected on a predetermined basis.

Sample forms for reporting nursing quality assurance monitoring activities are displayed in Exhibits 4-7, 4-8, and 4-9. Summary reports should include

- comparison of the data with the expected outcome
- the frequency with which a discrepancy in results occurred
- the action taken and status of resolution of identified discrepancies
- any information of interest that was found in addition to the problem or criteria monitored

### Meeting Minutes

Formal minutes of all nursing quality assurance committee meetings should be recorded. As in other meeting minutes, the meeting contents, problems or concerns identified, and the action recommended/taken to correct problems should be reflected. As with monitor results and quarterly summaries, copies of the minutes should be forwarded to nursing administration, the hospital quality assurance committee, and the appropriate hospital management. Support, recommendations, and action from administration and the medical executive committee are often needed to provide the action required to resolve problems. Exhibit 4-10 gives a sample format for documentation of meeting minutes.

Most hospitals require quarterly departmental quality assurance reports to the hospital quality assurance committee. In some cases regarding monitors of high priority, monthly reports are required. These reports should indicate the results of ongoing monitoring and appropriateness of care. The reports serve as a means of communicating and sharing quality monitoring activities with other disciplines through the hospital quality assurance committee. The sharing of results promotes interdisciplinary teamwork and heightens the awareness of quality assurance activities. Often, interdisciplinary involvement assists in the resolution of identified problems.

**Exhibit 4-7** Nursing Quality Assurance Monitors

| Standard | Monitor | Frequency of Data Collection | Expected Outcome Criteria | Method of Retrieval (Person[s] Responsible) |
|---|---|---|---|---|
| | | | | |

**Exhibit 4-8** Nursing Quality Assurance: Summary Report

Month(s)/Year

Check:
____ Monthly Summary
____ Quarterly Summary

| Monitor | Findings | Analysis | Action/Follow Up |
|---|---|---|---|
| | | | |

Exhibit 4-9 Nursing Quality Assurance Monitors: Summary

| Monitor | JUL | AUG | SEPT | OCT | NOV | DEC | JAN | FEB | MAR | APR | MAY | JUNE | ANNUAL |
|---------|-----|-----|------|-----|-----|-----|-----|-----|-----|-----|-----|------|--------|
|         |     |     |      |     |     |     |     |     |     |     |     |      |        |

**Exhibit 4-10** Sample Format for Documentation of Meeting Minutes

Nursing Quality Assurance Committee Meeting

Minutes for _____
                              Date

Attendance:

| Subject | Discussion | Action |
|---------|------------|--------|
|         |            |        |

## SUMMARY

The implementation of a nursing quality assurance program in rehabilitation involves nursing accountability and integration with other disciplines in the provision of quality and appropriate care. The focus is on appropriate patient outcomes—not merely that the patient got through the program, but how, and with what problems. Evaluation of monitors based on nursing standards of care gives nurses information about their performance in the provision of patient care.

The nursing quality assurance committee reviews monitors such as fall occurrences, nosocomial infection rates, medication variations, program evaluation, peer review, and patient satisfaction questionnaires in order to improve patient care. The selection of monitors involving high-priority topics is important—those that affect nursing care and appropriate patient outcomes, those having an effect on cost containment, and those that may result in increased liability. Quality assurance is not just counting, but preventing, changing, and improving. Evaluation of information derived from data collection and the reporting and resolution of problems identified from that information lead to a successful quality assurance program.

## NOTES

1. Mary Beth Harper Petersen, "Measuring Patient Satisfaction: Collecting Useful Data," *Journal of Nursing Quality Assurance* 2, no. 3 (May 1988): 26.

2. Alice Whittaker and Lauri McCanless, "Nursing Peer Review: Monitoring the Appropriateness and Outcome of Nursing Care," *Journal of Nursing Quality Assurance* 2, no. 2 (February 1988): 24–25.

3. Elizabeth Evans and Judith Heggie, "Implementing a Continuous Unit-Specific Quality Assurance Monitor," *Journal of Nursing Quality Assurance* 2, no. 2 (February 1988): 23.

4. Linda F. Maciorowski, "Quality Assurance Data: Whose Information Is It Anyway?" *Journal of Nursing Quality Assurance* 2, no. 3 (May 1988): 21.

5. Patricia S. Schroeder and Regina M. Maibusch, eds. *Nursing Quality Assurance: A Unit-Based Approach* (Rockville, Md.: Aspen Publishers, Inc., 1984), 224.

## BIBLIOGRAPHY

Beyerman, Kathleen. "Developing a Unit-Based Nursing Quality Assurance Program: From Concept to Practice." *Journal of Nursing Quality Assurance* 2 (1987): 1–11.

Commission on Accreditation of Rehabilitation Facilities. *Standards Manual for Organizations Serving People with Disabilities.* Tucson, Ariz.: Commission on Accreditation of Rehabilitation Facilities, 1987, 12–17, 29–39, 47.

Coyne, C., and Killien, M. "A System for Unit-Based Monitors of Quality of Nursing Care." *Journal of Nursing Administration* 17 (1987): 26–32.

Driever, Marie J. "Interpretation: A Critical Component of the Quality Assurance Process." *Journal of Nursing Quality Assurance* 2, no. 2 (February 1988): 55–58.

Ehrat, Karen S. "The Cost-Quality Balance: An Analysis of Quality, Effectiveness, Efficiency, and Cost." *Journal of Nursing Administration* 17 (1987): 6–13.

Evans, Elizabeth, and Heggie, Judith. "Implementing a Continuous Unit-Specific Quality Assurance Monitor." *Journal of Nursing Quality Assurance* 2, no. 2 (February 1988): 16–23.

Hamilton, Sharon. "Implementing a Successful Quality Assurance Program in the Rehabilitation Setting." *Journal of Nursing Quality Assurance* 2, no. 1 (November 1987): 49–57.

Isaac, Donald N. "Suggestions for Organizing a Quality Assurance Program." *Quality Review Bulletin* 9 (1983): 68–72.

Joint Commission on Accreditation of Healthcare Organizations. *Accreditation Manual for Hospitals, 1988.* Chicago: Joint Commission on Accreditation of Healthcare Organizations, 1988, 141–150.

Joint Commission on Accreditation of Healthcare Organizations. *Monitoring and Evaluation of the Quality and Appropriateness of Care.* Chicago: Joint Commission on Accreditation of Healthcare Organizations, 1986, 1–10.

Maciorowski, Linda F. "Quality Assurance Data: Whose Information Is It Anyway?" *Journal of Nursing Quality Assurance* 2, no. 3 (May 1988): 18–24.

Maciorowski, Linda F.; Larson, Elaine; and Keane, Anne. "Quality Assurance Evaluate Thyself." *Journal of Nursing Administration* 15, no. 6 (June 1985): 38–42.

Marx, Laurie, and Haskin, Joy. "Nursing QA: Step Two, Standards." *Journal of Quality Assurance* 10 (1988): 24–25.

Mason, D.J., and Daugherty, J.K. "Nursing Standards Should Determine Nursing's Price." *Nursing Management* 15 (1984): 34–38.

Meisenheimer, Claire Gavin. "Designing a QA Program." In *Quality Assurance—A Complete Guide to Effective Programs*, edited by Claire Gavin Meisenheimer. Rockville, Md.: Aspen Publishers, Inc., 1985.

Menzel, Ferol S., and Teegarden, Kathryn. "Quality Assurance: A Tri-Level Model." *Journal of Occupational Therapy* 36 (1982): 163–169.

Mumma, Christina M., ed. *Rehabilitation Nursing: Concepts and Practice—A Core Curriculum.* 2nd ed. Evanston, Ill.: Rehabilitation Nursing Foundation, 1987, 459–464.

Nadzam, Deborah M., and Atkins, Mardi. "The Pyramid for Quality Assurance." *Journal of Nursing Quality Assurance* 2, no. 1 (November 1987): 13–20.

Neubauer, Janice A.; Begley, Barbara; Jankowski, Becky Z.; and Keller, Kenneth. "Development and Implementation of Unit-Based Monitors." *Journal of Nursing Quality Assurance* 2, no. 2 (February 1988): 1–8.

O'Brien, Barbara L.; O'Such, Donald J.; and Pallette, Susan V. "Setting Realistic Goals for Quality Assurance Monitoring: Patient Falls versus Patient Days." *Quality Review Bulletin* (October 1987): 339–342.

Petersen, Mary Beth Harper. "Measuring Patient Satisfaction: Collecting Useful Data." *Journal of Nursing Quality Assurance* 2, no. 3 (May 1988): 25–35.

Poe, Stephanie S., and Will, Janet C. "Quality Nurse-Patient Outcomes: A Framework for Nursing Practice." *Journal of Nursing Quality Assurance* 2, no. 1 (November 1987): 29–37.

Poster, Elizabeth C., and Pelletier, Luc. "Primary versus Functional Medication Administration: Monitoring and Evaluating Medication Error Rates." *Journal of Nursing Quality Assurance* 2, no. 2 (February 1988): 68–76.

Seitz, Christine H., and Edwardson, Sandra R. "Nursing Care Costs for Stroke Patients in a Rehabilitation Setting." *Journal of Nursing Administration* 17 (1987): 17–22.

Sell, Heiner, and Goldstein, W.Z. "Evaluation, Not Revolution." *Quality Review Bulletin* (November 1978): 31–32.

Smeltzer, Carolyn H.; Feltman, Barbara; and Rajki, Karen. "Nursing Quality Assurance: A Process, Not a Tool." *Journal of Nursing Administration* 13, no. 1 (1983): 5–9.

Smith Marker, C.G. "The Marker Model: A Hierarchy for Nursing Standards." *Journal of Nursing Quality Assurance* 1, no. 2 (February 1987): 7–20.

Smith Marker, C.G. "Practical Tools for Quality Assurance: Criteria Development Sheet and Data Retrieval Form." *Journal of Nursing Quality Assurance* 2, no. 2 (February 1988): 43–54.

Tan, Marva West. "Problem Areas in Multidisciplinary Audit." *Quality Review Bulletin* 4 (November 1978): 33–35.

"Topics for Emergency Service Monitors." *QRC Advisor* 3 (1987): 1–6.

Whittaker, Alice, and McCanless, Lauri. "Nursing Peer Review: Monitoring the Appropriateness and Outcome of Nursing Care." *Journal of Nursing Quality Assurance* 2, no. 2 (February 1988): 24–31.

## SUGGESTED READINGS

Falvo, Donna R. *Effective Patient Education: A Guide to Increased Compliance.* Rockville, Md.: Aspen Publishers, Inc., 1985.

Ginsburg, Paul B., and Hammons, Glenn T. "Competition and the Quality of Care: The Importance of Information." *Hospital Management Review* 7, no. 6 (1988).

Graham, J. "Quality Gets a Closer Look." *Modern Health Care* (27 February 1987): 20–37.

Graham, Nancy O., ed. *Quality Assurance in Hospitals—Strategies for Assessment and Implementation*. Rockville, Md.: Aspen Publishers, Inc., 1982.

Griffith-Kenney, Janet W., and Christensen, Paula J., eds. *Nursing Process—Application of Theories, Frameworks and Models*. 2nd ed. St. Louis: C.V. Mosby Co., 1987.

Hamilton, Sharon, and Morales, Barbara J. "Unit-Level Quality Assurance: Essential for Success." *Rehabilitation Nursing* 13, no. 2 (1988), 76–78.

Martin, Nancy; Holt, Nancy B.; and Hicks, Dorothy, eds. *Comprehensive Rehabilitation Nursing*. New York: McGraw-Hill Book Co., 1981.

"Quality: Will It Make or Break Your Hospital?" *Hospitals* 5 (July 1986): 54–58.

Rowland, Howard S., and Rowland, Beatrice L., eds. *Nursing Administration Handbook*. 2nd ed. Rockville, Md.: Aspen Publishers, Inc., 1985.

Schroeder, Patricia S., and Maibusch, Regina M., eds. *Nursing Quality Assurance: A Unit-Based Approach*. Rockville, Md.: Aspen Publishers, Inc., 1984.

Stevens, Barbara J. *The Nurse As Executive*. 3rd ed. Rockville, Md.: Aspen Publishers, Inc., 1985.

Sullivan, Eleanor J., and Decker, Phillip J. *Effective Management in Nursing*. Menlo Park, Calif.: Addison-Wesley Publishing Co., Inc., 1985.

Wenzel, Richard P., ed. *Prevention and Control of Nosocomial Infections*. Baltimore: Williams & Wilkins Co., 1987.

Wysezewianski, Leon. "Quality of Care: Past Achievements and Future Challenges." *Hospital Management Review* 7, no. 6 (1988), 6.

# Chapter 5

# Evaluating Program Effectiveness

The essential element in any quality assurance program is evaluation. Health care services are being judged by a society that is experiencing spiraling health care costs as well as increasing federal government restraints on reimbursable health care expenses. Thus, a nursing quality assurance program must provide feedback useful for the development of cost-efficient health care programs.

Of course, the most important facet of evaluation relates to a program's influence on patient outcomes. Consumers, third party payers, and health care providers are carefully monitoring health care programs. When evaluating program effectiveness, rehabilitation nurses should ask themselves the following questions about the services they provide.

- Does the rehabilitation program impact on patient outcomes in the way intended?
- Is a measurement tool that is both valid and reliable used to measure the program's patient outcomes?
- Are the patients and families actively involved in setting goals and discharge planning? How is this documented?
- Is the program cost-effective? How is cost monitored?
- What is the nurse/patient ratio? Is it adequate? Is staffing determined by a valid and reliable patient classification system that is based on patient acuity?
- Are all levels of nursing staff who provide patient care involved in the quality assurance process?

## THE PURPOSE OF EVALUATION

The goal of the evaluation process is to collect data for the purpose of making a decision about nursing practice.[1] This process is value-laden, since its outcomes determine the worth of services provided. In most health care settings, however, evaluation data are useful only to the organization that performed the evaluation.[2] There are few, if any, attempts to generalize data to other organizations or patient groups. This is especially unfortunate for rehabilitation professionals who are currently involved in investigating various diagnosis-related group (DRG)-based case-mix approaches. An appropriate rehabilitation prospective payment system will be developed only if measures of patient characteristics, such as functional status, can be accurately generalized to patient groups. The need for generalization mandates that research be part of the evaluation process.

Research methodology can be incorporated into an evaluation study at any point in time. It is used to collect and analyze data for the purpose of studying a hypothesized relationship between two or more variables.[3] Research should be as free from bias as possible and, ideally, applicable to other patient groups.

An example of an evaluation question might be: Are nurses documenting nurse/patient collaborative rehabilitation goals within 48 hours of the patient's admission according to nursing department standards? The answer to this question would provide data regarding nursing adherence to a departmental standard.

A research hypothesis based on these data might be phrased as follows: Patients who are actively involved in planning their rehabilitation programs achieve significantly higher functional status scores on discharge than those who are not. Such a study would involve gathering information regarding patient involvement in goal planning and correlating it with data on discharge functional status scores. Research results might help nurses more successfully involve patients in planning their rehabilitation programs as well as promoting better patient outcomes. Thus, the evaluation process must include research as well as evaluation of organization or department standards if findings are to benefit the specialty as a whole.

**Table 5-1**  Pattern of Falls at a Rehabilitation Facility

| Unit* | January | February | March | April | May | June |
|---|---|---|---|---|---|---|
| SCI | 0 | 1 | 1 | 0 | 1 | 1 |
| CVA | 4 | 3 | 3 | 4 | 2 | 4 |
| Head injury | 3 | 3 | 4 | 3 | 3 | 2 |
| Orthopedic | 2 | 2 | 1 | 1 | 2 | 2 |
| Total | 9 | 9 | 9 | 8 | 8 | 9 |

*Each unit has a 30-bed capacity.

## PATTERNS VERSUS TRENDS

In order to evaluate nursing practice accurately, the nursing quality assurance committee must distinguish between patterns and trends in data. A *pattern* may be defined as "a mode of behavior regarded as characteristic of persons or things."[4] The key word is *characteristic*. When monitoring quality care, nurses should be familiar with the pattern of practice at their facilities. Table 5-1 illustrates a sample pattern of falls monitored at a hypothetical rehabilitation facility over a six-month period.

Each specialty unit consists of 30 beds, bringing census capacity to 120. There is an average of nine falls per month, and the head injury and cerebrovascular accident (CVA) units have a slightly higher number of falls on a monthly basis. Patients on these units may be at higher risk of falling as a result of neurological and cognitive deficits and, on the CVA unit, the greater age of the population. The nursing quality assurance committee, while continually promoting a decrease in the number of falls, is aware of the characteristic pattern of falls in its facility.

Table 5-2 illustrates the concept of a trend or a "current style or vogue"[5] within the same facility. Note that the orthopedic unit has shown a steady increase in its number of falls. This trend is particularly apparent when compared with the preceding six months (Table 5-1). Such a trend requires both reevaluation and aggressive action to remedy a possibly unsafe environment.

A "positive" trend also needs careful evaluation. For example, a unit displaying a steady decrease in the number of falls may be able to help other units by sharing actions taken to increase environmental safety. A "positive" trend, however, does not necessarily mean improvement. Consider the following scenario.

A 350-bed community hospital houses a 40-bed rehabilitation unit. This unit has the highest rate of falls in the hospital, averaging about two more per month than the acute care units. The majority of the patients are hospitalized for

**Table 5-2** Trend in Falls at a Rehabilitation Facility

| Unit* | July | August | September | October | November | December |
|-------|------|--------|-----------|---------|----------|----------|
| SCI | 0 | 1 | 1 | 1 | 0 | 1 |
| CVA | 3 | 3 | 4 | 4 | 3 | 2 |
| Head injury | 3 | 4 | 3 | 3 | 3 | 2 |
| Orthopedic | 2 | 3 | 4 | 4 | 5 | 5 |
| Total | 8 | 11 | 12 | 12 | 11 | 10 |

*Each unit has a 30-bed capacity.

rehabilitation after CVA. Over a three-month period of time, the number of falls on the rehabilitation unit has decreased markedly, so that the number of falls is averaging about two *less* per month than the acute care units. On paper, this trend looks wonderful. In reality, upon evaluation, it is a definite problem.

One month before the start of the new trend, the rehabilitation unit acquired a new head nurse, Ms. Evens. Ms. Evens had excellent managerial skills, but her background was strictly acute care. Upon her promotion Ms. Evens determined that one of her goals would be to decrease the incidence of falls on her unit and increase safety awareness. Inservices were held on safety issues, and the nursing staff began to exhibit more interest in promoting a safe patient environment. This result was positive. Unfortunately, as part of her concept of patient safety, Ms. Evens began to institute measures that curtailed patient independence.

Patients identified as at high risk of falling were encouraged to eat their meals in their rooms instead of making their way to the patients' dining room. The use of restraints increased. Assisting the patients to ambulate on the evening shift decreased. The patients' activities were curtailed in order to avoid falls. The rehabilitation program suffered.

Although safety awareness increased among certain staff members, achieving the rehabilitation goals of the patient and the team was hampered. Evaluation of this particular trend showed both positive and negative results of nursing interventions. Also shown was the importance of thoroughly evaluating *all* trends.

## PROGRAM EVALUATION

How can rehabilitation professionals be certain that their services are impacting on patient outcomes in the ways intended? How do nursing interventions influence the success of the rehabilitation program? The critical evaluation questions identified at the beginning of this chapter provide the basis for describing an effective method of program evaluation. The starting point, of course, is the measurement of patient outcomes.

### Patient Outcomes

There is a variety of measurement tools available with which to measure patients' functional abilities. Examples include the Functional Independence Measure (FIM), designed to measure what the patient is actually able to do,[6] and the LORS American Data System (LADS), which is a corporate-owned, integrated reporting system for inpatient rehabilitation.[7] Regardless of the instrument selected, several guidelines must be followed if program evaluation is to be effective.

- The measurement tool should be both valid and reliable.
- The tool should be able to assess accurately the status of the facility's/unit's rehabilitation patients.
- All members of the interdisciplinary team should be well versed in the purpose and use of the instrument. The team must be consistent when assessing outcomes.
- A formalized method of program evaluation must be established and results shared with the team.
- The interdisciplinary team must be involved in both reviewing patient outcome and making recommendations for improvements in patient services.
- The effectiveness of corrective actions should be assessed, and improvements in quality *must* be documented.

The Commission on Accreditation of Rehabilitation Facilities (CARF) publishes a manual to assist rehabilitation facilities/units in the development of a useful format for program evaluation.[8] Again, as in selection of a patient outcome measurement tool, the most important point is to utilize a system that "fits" program needs and with which the interdisciplinary team is familiar.

Table 5-3 illustrates a sample set of program evaluation data. The objective to increase independence in mobility did not meet the established criterion of 85 percent. How does the interdisciplinary team in general, and nursing in particular, investigate this problem?

Patients' mobility status during the month of April must be assessed. Were patients suffering especially disabling injuries as compared with the previous months? Did medical complications hinder progress in the rehabilitation program? Was the entire team consistent in its therapeutic approach to enhance mobility status? In particular, was nursing consistent in its mobility approaches throughout all three shifts? This last question is of especial importance to nursing quality assurance. Without nursing's 24-hour follow-through, maximizing a patient's mobility status is not possible.

Although program evaluation is an interdisciplinary effort, each discipline must evaluate its individual performance as it contributes to the entire program. The nursing quality assurance plan should include monitors that help to assess nursing services as components of interdisciplinary programs.

### Patient/Family Involvement in Goal Planning

An essential requirement of any rehabilitation program is that the patient and his or her family are actively involved in establishing goals and planning care.

**Table 5-3** Sample Program Evaluation Format: Head Injury Program, April 1988

| Objective | Population | Criteria | | How Measured | Achievement |
|---|---|---|---|---|---|
| | | Goal | Optimal | | |
| Increase independence in self-care skills by discharge | All patients not independent in self-care skills upon admission | 85% | 100% | Patient outcome measurement tool | 90% |
| Increase independence in bowel/bladder care by discharge | All patients not independent in bowel/bladder care upon admission | 85% | 100% | Patient outcome measurement tool | 90% |
| Increase independence in mobility by discharge | All patients not independent in mobility upon admission | 85% | 100% | Patient outcome measurement tool | 80% |
| Avoid institutionalization at discharge | All patients | 85% | 100% | Discharge destination | 85% |

The interdisciplinary team must document how this involvement is accomplished throughout the patient's hospitalization. Nursing quality assurance is primarily concerned with nursing's mutuality of nurse/patient/family goal establishment and its documentation. The following guidelines should assist the nursing department in this process.

- Patient/family goals should be identified within the first 48 hours of the patient's admission. Ideally, goals are assessed during the admission process, documented on an admission assessment form, and are part of the patient care plan.

- If the patient is unable to communicate (either verbally or in writing) the family should be utilized as a major resource for establishing goals. It may be necessary to interview the family by telephone, depending upon availability, but every effort must be made to note patient/family concerns and objectives for rehabilitation.

- If it is not possible to identify patient goals initially (for example, because of the patient's cognitive status) and family or friends are unavailable (or do not exist), nursing should document the problems pertaining to patient goal identification. Follow-up documentation should include efforts to involve the patient in planning care as well as the involvement of any family and friends who may begin to participate in the rehabilitation process.

- Another source of information regarding patient/family goals and concerns is the acute care health professionals who worked with the patient prior to transfer to rehabilitation services. They may be able to help in identifying the family "leader" and patient/family concerns during the acute phase of illness or injury. Likewise, community health professionals, if involved in the patient's care prior to rehabilitation, may be of invaluable assistance in planning care and identifying patient/family goals.

## Staffing

Rehabilitation patient acuity and the corresponding nursing workload are increasing. Staffing should be determined by a valid and reliable patient classification system that is based on patient acuity. Staffing issues impact heavily on program services that cannot be effectively delivered without adequate personnel. A meaningful patient classification system "supplies the tools necessary to provide and justify adequate and appropriately skilled nursing staff to meet the standards for quality and appropriateness of nursing care."[9]

Issues in nursing management, such as the patient classification system and corresponding staffing needs, should be monitored by the nursing quality assurance committee. Rehabilitation is a specialty founded on the interdisciplinary team concept. Nursing staffing issues impact not only on nursing services, but on the team's services as well. When evaluating the effectiveness of nursing care, the nursing quality assurance committee must be aware of nurse management issues as well as those of direct clinical practice. Nursing personnel should be well versed in the facility's acuity system so that accurate, consistent ratings of patient acuity are determined.

## Marketing

A written marketing plan is part of the planning process when developing rehabilitation programs. According to CARF, the marketing plan "should be based upon the results of the organization's investigations and its mission in the community."[10] Marketing objectives should be established, as well as mechanisms to specify target audiences, and a means to identify necessary marketing changes due to consumer needs. A communications plan that identifies vehicles for communicating available services to the public should be established.[11]

The achievement of marketing objectives is a quality assurance issue that affects the delivery of all rehabilitation services. Nursing quality assurance should be aware of the answers to the following questions.

- Is the marketing plan communicated effectively to identified target audiences? How is this measured? Is the cost of services part of the plan?
- How are consumer needs assessed so that viable changes are made in both the marketing plan and program services?
- Are specific rehabilitation programs (head injury, stroke) marketed individually? If so, are the interdisciplinary teams involved in the marketing plans?

Nursing's involvement in the marketing process is critical to its success. Because they are responsible for 24-hour continuity of care, nurses are in a position to identify marketing concepts from an "around-the-clock" viewpoint. Nursing quality assurance should be interested in monitoring nursing's involvement in the marketing process and its influence on assessing the impact on target audiences.

## THE EVALUATION PROCESS

The evaluation process, although detailed, need not be confusing or needlessly complex. The following examples of nursing quality assurance evaluations have been divided into three categories: (1) nursing quality assurance within a free-standing rehabilitation facility, (2) nursing quality assurance on a rehabilitation unit located within an acute care facility, and (3) nursing quality assurance as part of program evaluation.

### Free-Standing Rehabilitation Facility

Table 5-4 illustrates a portion of a quarterly nursing quality assurance report from a hypothetical 88-bed rehabilitation facility. Upon analysis of findings, the nursing quality assurance committee noted that in August and September the criterion for "patient goals documented within 48 hours of admission" was not achieved. The committee's first step was to analyze the findings on a unit level (Table 5-5).

The rehabilitation hospital contains four 22-bed specialty units: stroke (CVA), spinal cord injury (SCI), head injury, and pain management. Upon analysis, the only unit deficient in meeting the 100 percent criterion was the CVA unit. The nurse representative from the CVA unit reviewed the medical records of the seven patients whose goals were not identified. Prior to the review, the nursing quality assurance committee identified pertinent data to be obtained.

- Was the patient alert and oriented within the first 48 hours after admission?
- Was the patient able to communicate effectively either verbally or in writing? Was he or she able to comprehend spoken and/or written communication?
- Were family and friends used as resources for goal identification?
- If the patient was transferred from an acute care facility, were the health care professionals from that facility used as resources?
- What was the level of stroke rehabilitation expertise of the nurses providing care for the first 48 hours after admission?

Table 5-6 illustrates results of the chart review. This information was presented during a nursing quality assurance meeting at which the nurse manager of the CVA unit was an invited guest. Four of seven patients were admitted and cared for by nurses from the facility's float pool for the first 48 hours of hospitalization on the day and evening shifts (a total of eight different nurses). Although the patients received their care from the same float pool nurses for those 48 hours, none of the nurses had ever provided care to such recently admitted stroke patients in a rehabilitation facility. Additionally, three of the eight float pool nurses had never worked on the CVA unit prior to that time. Finally, the float pool was a recent addition (July 1988) to the facility's nursing staff.

**Table 5-4** Quarterly Nursing Quality Assurance Report: July, August, and September 1988

| Monitor | Criterion | Findings | Analysis | Action |
|---|---|---|---|---|
| Number of medication errors per month | Less than 3 | July, 2<br>August, 1<br>September, 1 | Criterion met<br>Criterion met<br>Criterion met | Continue monitoring<br>Continue monitoring<br>Continue monitoring |
| Number of patient falls per month | Less than 10 | July, 8<br>August, 8<br>September, 9 | Criterion met<br>Criterion met<br>Criterion met | Continue monitoring<br>Continue monitoring<br>Continue monitoring |
| Number of primary nurse follow-up phone calls two weeks post-discharge (%) | 100% | July, 100%<br>August, 100%<br>September, 100% | Criterion met<br>Criterion met<br>Criterion met | Continue monitoring<br>Continue monitoring<br>Continue monitoring |
| Number of patient goals documented within 48 hours of admission (%) | 100% | July, 100%<br>August, 95%<br>September, 88% | Criterion met<br>Failed to meet criterion<br>Failed to meet criterion | Continue monitoring<br>August/September findings plan:<br>1. Analyze data on unit level<br>2. Review charts of patients whose goals were not identified within 48 hours<br>3. Share results with nursing administration team and recommend action |

**Table 5-5** Analysis of Findings by Unit

| Unit | Number of Admissions | Number of Patients with Identified Goals |
|------|---------------------|------------------------------------------|
| | *August 1988* | |
| CVA | 10 | 8 (80%) |
| Head injury | 12 | 12 (100%) |
| SCI | 8 | 8 (100%) |
| Pain management | 10 | 10 (100%) |

Total number of admissions = 40
Total number of patients with identified goals within 48 hours = 38 (95%)

| | September 1988 | |
|------|---------------------|------------------------------------------|
| CVA | 11 | 6 (55%) |
| Head injury | 11 | 11 (100%) |
| SCI | 10 | 10 (100%) |
| Pain management | 9 | 9 (100%) |

Total number of admissions = 41
Total number of patients with identified goals within 48 hours = 36 (88%)

Analysis of patient characteristics showed that four of the seven patients were not alert and oriented upon admission, and all seven had some difficulty with either verbal or written communication and comprehension of communication. Family, friends, and previous caregivers were not used as goal identification resources.

The analysis of findings seemed to reveal two distinct problems: nursing's use of alternative methods of patient goal identification and the readiness of the float pool staff to admit stroke patients. The chairperson of the nursing quality assurance committee, the committee's CVA unit representative, primary nurses from all three shifts on the CVA unit, two float pool nurses (both of whom were involved in the analyzed admission), and the director of staff development (responsible for orientation) met to recommend action for problem resolution.

## Float Pool Concerns

The following concerns were identified by the float pool representatives.

- insufficient orientation time
- lack of support from the regular staff when assigned to the stroke unit (insufficient information about patient assignments, little or no assistance in

**Table 5-6** Chart Review for Lack of Goal Identification in CVA Patients (within 48 Hours of Admission)

| Patient | Alert/Oriented | Communication | | Comprehension | | Resources Used | | Nursing CVA Rehabilitation Experience |
| --- | --- | --- | --- | --- | --- | --- | --- | --- |
| | | Verbal | Written | Verbal | Written | Family and Friends | Acute Care | |
| 1 | Yes | No | Yes | Yes | Yes | No | No | Float pool (D,E)* |
| 2 | No | No | No | No | ?† | No | No | Regular staff |
| 3 | No | No | ? | Yes | ? | ? | No | Regular staff |
| 4 | Yes | Yes | No | Yes | Yes | No | No | Float pool (D,E) |
| 5 | No | No | ? | No | ? | ? | ? | Float pool (D,E) |
| 6 | Yes | No | Yes | Yes | Yes | ? | No | Regular staff |
| 7 | No | No | ? | Yes | ? | No | No | Float pool (D,E) |

*D = day shift; E = evening shift.
†A question mark indicates unknown or unable to assist.

locating supplies and equipment)

- insufficient inservicing on assessment methods for the disoriented patient and for the patient experiencing difficulty in communication

*Regular Staff Concerns*

- the float pool's unpreparedness in stroke rehabilitation nursing
- "not enough time" to perform adequate admission assessments and interventions
- the feeling that certain members of the float pool should be assigned only to specific areas

*Recommended Action: Float Pool and Staff Development*

After reviewing orientation costs and staffing needs, it was decided that orientation time could not be increased. Additionally, the float pool nurses themselves were not available for a more lengthy orientation schedule. Although it would be ideal to orient float pool nurses exclusively for certain areas, staffing needs necessitated that float pool nurses work on all areas. The following steps were taken to improve orientation.

- The orientation content was revised so that more time was devoted to specific rehabilitation interventions for each of the four specialty areas.
- Self-learning packets were developed for each of the four specialty areas with special emphasis on admission procedures. Continuing educational units (CEUs) were obtained for the packets as well as financial compensation awarded for packet completion. Completion was done outside the facility. The maximal time for completion was 1.5 hours for each packet.
- The orientation included a tour of each unit with emphasis on location of key supplies and equipment.

*Recommended Action: CVA Unit Staff*

The nurse manager discussed concerns with all levels of the unit staff. The group acknowledged the importance of providing sufficient information on unit routines and patient needs to float pool nurses. Time constraints, when providing care, were a genuine concern, and the staff initiated the following actions in an attempt to resolve problems.

- An assignment sheet form was developed with input from both staff development and float pool personnel. The form was designed to highlight information essential to adequate patient care and to facilitate location of unit supplies.

- Whenever possible, float pool nurses would not be responsible for patient admissions.
- Methods of assigning patient caseloads were reviewed. The patients requiring the most complex care would, whenever possible, be the responsibility of regular staff. Float pool nurses could provide care to a greater number of patients, thus balancing the workload.
- A recommendation was sent to the nursing administration team to simplify the nursing admission process. A committee was established to work on this problem.
- It was decided that assessment of verbal and written communication should be incorporated as part of the CVA unit admission process.
- Resources other than the patient, if necessary, would be used for goal identification (i.e., family, friends, previous health care providers), and continuing efforts to involve the patient in the plan of care would be documented.

### Reevaluation of the Problem

The nursing quality assurance committee had the responsibility of evaluating the effectiveness of the recommended actions. In addition to continuing to monitor the number of patient goals documented within 48 hours of admission, the committee decided to

- monitor the number of float pool nurses who successfully completed the orientation self-learning packets within the identified time frame
- randomly review the number of patient caseload assignments, considering both patient needs and appropriate utilization of float pool personnel

As often happens in the quality assurance process, the identification of one problem may lead to the discovery of others. It is hoped that recommended action will enhance both patient care and professional growth.

## Rehabilitation Unit within an Acute Care Facility

A partial listing of nursing quality assurance data from a fictitious 350-bed community hospital is listed in Table 5-7. Falls have exceeded the established criterion. Upon investigation, it was found that the 35-bed general rehabilitation unit had been experiencing an increase in the number of falls taking place over the past three months (Table 5-8).

Analysis of data from the rehabilitation unit showed several patterns (Table 5-9). Of the 23 patients who fell, 12 (56 percent) had had a stroke, and 6 patients (26

**Table 5-7** Community Hospital Nursing Quality Assurance Results: Quarterly Report, Second Quarter, 1988

| Monitor | Criterion | Findings | Analysis | Action |
|---------|-----------|----------|----------|--------|
| Number of medication errors per month | Less than 12 | April, 11<br>May, 10<br>June, 10 | Criterion achieved<br>Criterion achieved<br>Criterion achieved | Continue to monitor<br>Continue to monitor<br>Continue to monitor |
| Number of decubitus ulcers developed per month | 0 | April, 0<br>May, 0<br>June, 0 | Criterion achieved<br>Criterion achieved<br>Criterion achieved | Continue to monitor<br>Continue to monitor<br>Continue to monitor |
| Number of IV infiltrations per month | 0 | April, 0<br>May, 0<br>June, 0 | Criterion achieved<br>Criterion achieved<br>Criterion achieved | Continue to monitor<br>Continue to monitor<br>Continue to monitor |
| Number of falls on nursing units per month | Less than 20 | April, 21<br>May, 25<br>June, 28 | Established criterion was exceeded throughout quarter | 1. Analyze falls by unit<br>2. Review circumstances surrounding falls<br>3. Make recommendations |

**Table 5-8** Number of Falls by Unit during the Second Quarter, 1988

| Unit | April | May | June |
|------|-------|-----|------|
| 2 West | 2 | 0 | 1 |
| 2 East | 4 | 4 | 4 |
| 3 North | 0 | 2 | 3 |
| 3 West | 3 | 2 | 2 |
| 3 East | 4 | 2 | 3 |
| **4 North (rehabilitation)** | 5 | 9 | 9 |
| 4 West | 1 | 2 | 2 |
| 4 East | 2 | 3 | 3 |
| Intensive care | 0 | 1 | 0 |
| Critical care | 0 | 0 | 1 |
| Total | 21 | 25 | 28 |

percent) had had a below-the-knee amputation. This was consistent with the average population of the unit on a monthly basis, the two most frequently occurring admitting diagnoses being CVA and below-the-knee amputation. Of the 23 patients, 18 (78 percent) were over 50 years of age. Again, this was consistent with the age ranges of the unit population in general.

There were no identifiable patterns in the sex of the patients, the day of the week, or date of the month when falls took place. The two most significant results of data analysis were in the areas of time and type of occurrence. Fourteen of the falls (61 percent) took place during the hours of 4:00 P.M. and 6:00 P.M. Thirteen of the falls (57 percent) took place while the patients were attempting to transfer to or from a wheelchair.

The nursing quality assurance committee's rehabilitation unit representative shared these data with the unit's staff and nurse manager. The staff first identified what they felt to be several factors that contributed to the unacceptable fall rates.

- There was a shortage of staff on the 3:00–11:00 P.M. shift.
- The staff felt "rushed and pressured" during the hours of 4:00–6:00 P.M., when patients needed to receive 4:00 P.M. medications and treatments and be helped to the patients' dining room for supper.
- Agency and "float pool" personnel were employed who were unfamiliar with transfer and bed mobility techniques used on the rehabilitation unit.
- The patients' suppers were delivered at 5:30 P.M., when one-half of the nursing staff were on their own supper breaks.
- The nursing department traditionally staffed all units by allocating the most personnel on the day shift. The rehabilitation unit staff felt that more

**Table 5-9** Fall Analysis: Second Quarter, 1988

| Patient | Diagnosis* | Age | Sex | Time | Day | Date | Type |
|---------|-----------|-----|-----|------|-----|------|------|
| | | | | *April 1988* | | | |
| 1 | CVA | 67 | M | 4:30 P.M. | Friday | 4/8 | T* |
| 2 | CVA | 74 | F | 5:15 P.M. | Sunday | 4/17 | FL |
| 3 | R BKA | 62 | M | 5:30 P.M. | Tuesday | 4/5 | FL |
| 4 | HI | 25 | M | 10:00 A.M. | Monday | 4/11 | W |
| 5 | CVA | 70 | F | 4:00 P.M. | Wednesday | 4/20 | T |
| | | | | *May 1988* | | | |
| 1 | L BKA | 80 | M | 4:00 P.M. | Monday | 5/9 | T |
| 2 | CVA | 78 | M | 10:00 P.M. | Tuesday | 5/2 | W |
| 3 | HI | 22 | F | 9:00 A.M. | Tuesday | 5/17 | FL |
| 4 | L BKA | 55 | F | 9:00 P.M. | Saturday | 5/21 | T |
| 5 | MS | 45 | F | 2:00 P.M. | Friday | 5/27 | W |
| 6 | CVA | 65 | M | 5:00 P.M. | Thursday | 5/5 | T |
| 7 | CVA | 72 | M | 9:30 P.M. | Wednesday | 5/18 | W |
| 8 | R BKA | 51 | F | 4:45 P.M. | Monday | 5/25 | T |
| 9 | CVA | 64 | M | 4:30 P.M. | Sunday | 5/29 | T |
| | | | | *June 1988* | | | |
| 1. | CVA | 73 | F | 4:00 P.M. | Sunday | 6/5 | T |
| 2 | CVA | 60 | M | 5:00 P.M. | Sunday | 6/19 | W |
| 3 | R BKA | 88 | M | 5:30 P.M. | Tuesday | 6/21 | T |
| 4. | CVA | 55 | F | 9:15 P.M. | Wednesday | 6/22 | T |
| 5 | CVA | 64 | F | 10:00 A.M. | Monday | 6/27 | W |
| 6 | HI | 30 | F | 6:00 P.M. | Thursday | 6/30 | T |
| 7 | R BKA | 55 | M | 2:00 P.M. | Friday | 6/10 | FL |
| 8 | HI | 32 | F | 4:30 P.M. | Tuesday | 6/28 | T |
| 9 | CVA | 80 | M | 5:15 P.M. | Saturday | 6/18 | T |

*Key: BKA, below-the-knee amputee; FL, found on floor; HI, head injury; MS, multiple sclerosis; T, fell while transferring to or from wheelchair; W, fell while walking.

personnel should be assigned to the evening shift than to the day shift, since a great deal of the patient education, as well as showering patients, was accomplished in the evening.

With the support and assistance of the nursing quality assurance committee, a plan for problem resolution was developed by the rehabilitation unit staff. Several proposed interventions would take considerable time to implement. Thus, the nurse manager instituted the following innovations immediately.

- Staff schedules were arranged so that two nurses worked a "split shift" (10:00 A.M.–6:30 P.M.) to help assist patients with their treatment and medication regimens and preparations for supper.
- Arrangements were made with the dietary department to have patients' supper trays delivered at 6:00 P.M. instead of 5:30 P.M. Most nurses would have finished their own meals and returned to the unit by 5:30 P.M. This would make the whole staff available for assistance with the patients' supper.
- With the assistance of the staff development department and the rehabilitation clinical nurse specialist, inservices on transfer and bed mobility technique were instituted for the float pool staff. Regular reviews on the same techniques were instituted for the regular rehabilitation staff as well.

Interviewing, which would require a more lengthy period of implementation, was also instituted.

- The nurse manager of the rehabilitation unit reevaluated the methods utilized to calculate patient acuity and the resulting staffing needs. After paying special attention to the educational and activities of daily living skills taking place on the evening shift, a proposal was made to nursing administration requesting reallocation of staff to the 3:00–11:00 P.M. shift.
- Staff nurses developed a system of peer review in order to monitor safety on the unit. Especially important factors were transfer techniques, body mechanics, assisting patients with bed positioning, bed mobility, and activities of daily living. This system was incorporated into the nursing quality assurance system.

*Reevaluation of the Problem*

The effectiveness of the interventions was monitored by the unit staff within the first two weeks of implementation. Although the primary concern was the incidence of falls, it was also important to note the impact of the interventions on staffing adequacy. Equally important was the impact on the dietary department, which had made innovations of its own in order to assist the rehabilitation unit. Nursing quality assurance is seldom, if ever, isolated within its own department.

The nursing quality assurance committee received a positive report from the rehabilitation unit representative at its next meeting. Falls had decreased from nine to six within one month. The staff reported an increase in time spent with patients when teaching transfer techniques and other activities of daily living. Still to be evaluated were the effects of inservice training for the float pool staff, the transfer technique review classes held for the regular staff, and nursing administration's response to the proposed reallocation of staff. Clearly, it would take several months to evaluate properly the effectiveness of the interventions. In summary, the nursing quality assurance committee, in conjunction with the rehabilitation nursing staff, would monitor

- incidence and circumstances of falls
- effects of inservice training
- patient acuity and staffing patterns
- peer review of safety practices

**Quality Assurance and Program Evaluation**

A 200-bed free-standing rehabilitation facility has recently opened a 30-bed SCI unit. A portion of its program evaluation is given in Table 5-10. After three months of evaluation, it became apparent that the objective regarding achievement of 90 percent on the written post-test would have to be reevaluated. The percentages of patients meeting the objective in the first three months were as follows: Month 1, 90 percent; Month 2, 88 percent; Month 3, 87 percent. The established criterion was a 96 percent achievement rate. The SCI team decided on the following actions to evaluate the problem.

- Review the content of the patient education series as a team and within the individual disciplines responsible for each content area.
- Request the assistance of the education department in evaluating both the content and methods of presentation.
- Develop a format for the patients and families to evaluate the patient education series.
- Ask the quality assurance department for recommendations in establishing appropriate educational monitors.

*Content Review*

The lecture content of the patient education series included

| Topic | Speaker(s) |
|---|---|
| Anatomy and Physiology of SCI | Medicine and Nursing |
| Activities of Daily Living | Physical and Occupational Therapies |
| Bladder and Bowel Management | Nursing |
| Skin Care | Nursing |
| Nutrition | Dietary |
| Sexuality | Psychology |
| Coping with Emergencies | Nursing |
| Leisure Counseling | Therapeutic Recreation |

**Table 5-10** SCI Program Evaluation

| Objective | Population | Criteria | | How Measured |
| --- | --- | --- | --- | --- |
| | | Goal | Optimal | |
| Increase independence in self-care skills by discharge | All patients/families not independent upon admission | 90% | 100% | Outcome measurement tool |
| Increase independence in bowel/bladder care by discharge | All patients/families not independent upon admission | 90% | 100% | Outcome measurement tool |
| Achieve a score of 90% on written portion of post-test upon completion of the lecture component patient education series | All patients/families | 96% | 100% | Post-test score on written examination |
| Achieve a passing score on return demonstration of activities of daily living skills upon completion of patient education series | All patients/families | 100% | 100% | Return demonstration of activities of daily living skills |

Two classes were taught per week. Each class was one hour in length. All speakers utilized extensive handouts and audiovisual aids. The eight classes were completed within one month. The speakers were consistent from month to month with the exception of the nursing department, whose speakers varied from month to month.

### Education Department

After reviewing the content and attending the educational presentations, the representatives from the education department made a number of critical observations. First, both verbal and written content had been prepared on a high school graduate level. There were, however, a significant number of patients and families who did not have the reading and speaking skills of a high school graduate. Second, there was a great deal of information presented in a single session, and little opportunity for the participants to ask questions. Also, the presenters' teaching skills varied greatly. Third, it was noted that the patients and their families had little or no difficulty in the return demonstration areas of the patient education series. These skills were often taught on a one-to-one basis with frequent repetitions and ample opportunity for patients to ask questions. Additionally, these skills were reinforced daily by all interdisciplinary team members. Finally, there was no mechanism for participant evaluation of the education series.

### Patient/Family Feedback

Patients and families who had already completed the patient education series were contacted. Most felt the content was valuable, but stated that there was "too much information covered too quickly." They found actual visual demonstration the most effective teaching method, and found video presentations quite beneficial.

### Quality Assurance Feedback

The SCI unit's nursing quality assurance representative (at the team's request) consulted with the nursing quality assurance chairperson. The newness of both the education series and the unit itself made establishing criteria especially challenging. The chairperson recommended surveying other SCI units regarding educational programs and program evaluation establishment.

### Actions

- Simplify the content of lecture presentations.
    1. Modify the lecture content and written material so that persons reading at the seventh grade level or above could comprehend information.

2. Identify a maximum of two measurable objectives to be achieved at the end of each one-hour presentation.

3. Limit handouts to the areas that concern identified objectives. Inform audiences that additional materials are readily available from the staff if desired. (This should be assessed on an individual basis.)

4. Keep the actual lecture content or video presentations to a 45-minute time period, thus ensuring a 15-minute period for questions and answers.

5. Base the lecture content (as much as possible) on an actual visual demonstration (e.g., skin checks, bed mobility).

6. Present only one class per week, thus allowing time for comprehension of content. This will expand the educational series from one to two months. Since the average length of stay is ten weeks, there should be an opportunity for participants to attend each class.

7. Split the bowel and bladder lecture into two separate presentations. These areas have too much information for a single presentation.

8. Construct the post-test at the same reading and verbal comprehension level as the lecture presentations. A staff member should be available during the test to clarify questions as necessary.

9. Each department will identify a maximum of two speakers to present content. These persons not only should be knowledgeable in the content area but should possess the necessary speaking and educational skills as well. The education department will offer assistance in speaker identification as well as help additional staff persons become skilled in the teacher role.

- Develop a format for patient/family evaluation of the education series.

1. At the end of each one-hour session a *brief* (no more than six questions) evaluation form will be given to each participant to complete. Staff members will be available to assist as necessary. This will provide immediate feedback for the instructors. A single evaluation form covering all eight classes should be avoided. This is often confusing for patients and provides inaccurate data because of the time gaps between sessions and evaluation.

2. The results of these evaluations will be shared monthly with the interdisciplinary team, and actions will be recommended for continual improvement in the educational series.

- Reassess monitors and criteria established.

1. Continue to monitor scores on all areas of patient educational testing. However, review six months of data prior to establishing criteria. This will allow needed evaluation time since the program itself is so new.

In summary, nursing quality assurance impacts on all phases of evaluation, regardless of setting. The nursing quality assurance committee in a rehabilitation setting also must be aware of its influence in the interdisciplinary program evaluation and plan its program accordingly.

## RESEARCH AND NURSING QUALITY ASSURANCE

Nursing quality assurance activities may generate or increase nursing research being conducted by a facility. Corrective actions may lead to exploration of a particular problem's various solutions. This, in turn, could lead to the study of a hypothesis proposing a relationship between two or more variables. How is it possible to generate a sound research study from quality assurance activities?

The first step would be to seek out expert counseling. Nurse-researchers are becoming increasingly more available to administrative and staff nurses alike. Research positions within a nursing department, liaison roles with faculty-researchers from university settings, and research consultants are a few of the resources available when designing a research project.

Second, the staff nurses' cooperation and interest in clinical research must be established. There are two frequently occurring problems in clinical research.

1. a nurse-researcher who may expect the clinical nurses to give priority to a study instead of to patient care
2. patients who may become involved in multiple studies, causing lengthy, frequent interruptions in patient care[12]

In order to avoid these common problems and develop sound studies, investigators must recognize the efforts of the staff nurse and encourage involvement. To spark interest in the research process, the nursing quality assurance committee may begin by presenting a recent research study that is relevant to a problem being evaluated by the nursing department. Discussion of such relevant studies may become a regular nursing quality assurance activity. Such strategies are most effective when the studies under discussion are directly related to a particular patient problem.

As interest in research grows, the identified expert or resource person may be invited to help the staff nurses clarify their ideas for investigation. Again, involvement of the staff is critical to the success of any study. Once a problem has been identified, the next logical step is hypothesis development.

## Developing a Research Project

The nurses on an SCI unit in a 150-bed rehabilitation facility (Rehab A) have taught their patients to perform self-catheterization using a clean technique instead of a sterile technique. The patients experience a very low rate of urinary tract infections, and the nurses believe that the ease of the clean technique is a factor contributing to this low incidence.

However, SCI nurses at a sister facility (Rehab B) within the same corporation believe just as strongly in teaching patients to perform self-catheterization using the sterile technique. The corporation administrators have decided that nursing procedures need to be as consistent as possible. Thus, Rehab A's nurses decide that a research investigation will help to prove their case for the clean technique.

Rehab A hypothesized that patients performing self-catheterization using the clean technique will experience fewer urinary tract infections than patients using the sterile technique while hospitalized. In order to test this hypothesis, a sample of patients using the sterile technique must be found. Thus, Rehab B nurses were asked to participate in the investigation. Eager to have their viewpoint proven correct, they agreed to participate.

A literature review was done to gather current information on SCI and self-catheterization techniques. Representatives from each facility met to clarify the following points.

- time span of the investigation and sample size
- patient characteristics (In order to control for as many variables as possible, age range, level of SCI, and ability to perform procedures were considered when deciding which patients would be part of the sample.)
- protocols for self-catheterization (Protocols from each facility were examined to ensure as much consistency as possible [i.e., What level of nursing personnel would be teaching the procedure? What were the guidelines for frequency of self-catheterization, fluid restrictions, diagnostic evaluations, and assessment of patients' readiness to learn?])

Nursing quality assurance representatives and the infection control nurse would provide data concerning the rate of urinary tract infections. Weekly tests for urine culture and sensitivity were already a part of the self-catheterization protocol at each facility. Results of the urine laboratory studies were the primary source of data. Data were collected and analyzed with the help of the nursing quality assurance committee.

Throughout the investigation, other questions surfaced. What was the incidence of urinary tract infections after discharge? Did infections result in time lost from work or school? What was the incidence of urinary tract infection in high-level injury patients whose caregivers had to perform the catheterizations? How would the results of the study be shared with the remaining corporation facilities? How would the results be formulated into policy?

Research, as in any evaluation process, tends to generate at least as many questions as answers. This hypothetical initiation of a research project illustrates how nursing quality assurance may promote and assist in nursing investigations.

## SUMMARY

The process of evaluating the outcomes of nursing care is the most critical aspect of nursing quality assurance. In rehabilitation nursing, this process involves not only nursing, but its impact on interdisciplinary team functioning as well. Whether services are provided in a free-standing facility or on a rehabilitation unit within an acute care facility, the results of nursing quality assurance activities must be utilized to enhance and improve patient care and nursing services. These results also should be evaluated in terms of interdisciplinary program evaluation.

The research process can be initiated and promoted by nursing quality assurance activities. The results of a properly conducted investigation may be used to generalize findings to a specific rehabilitation population and ultimately improve services to these persons. Regardless of methodology, both evaluation and research are critical components of a sound nursing quality assurance program.

---

### NOTES

1. W. James Popham, *Educational Evaluation* (Englewood Cliffs, N.J.: Prentice-Hall, 1975), 34.

2. Walter Borg and Meridith Gall, *Educational Research*, 3rd ed. (New York: Longman Publishing, 1979), 601.

3. Cathleen Krueger Wilson, "Program Evaluation: Theory, Method, and Practice," in *Nursing Quality Assurance: A Unit-Based Approach*, eds. Patricia S. Schroeder and Regina M. Maibusch (Rockville, Md.: Aspen Publishers, Inc., 1984), 207.

4. Jess Stern, ed., *Random House Dictionary* (New York: Random House, Inc., 1978), 658.

5. Ibid., 939.

6. Functional Independence Measure (FIM), developed by Carl Granger, M.D. Sponsored by the American Congress of Rehabilitation Medicine and the American Academy of Physical Medicine and Rehabilitation. Supported by a grant from the National Institute of Handicapped Research. Copyright 1986, Uniform Data System for Medical Rehabilitation.

7. Raymond G. Carey and Jerry H. Seibert, "Integrating Program Evaluation, Quality Assurance, and Marketing for Inpatient Rehabilitation," *Rehabilitation Nursing* 13 (1988): 66–70.

8. Commission on Accreditation of Rehabilitation Facilities, *Program Evaluation in Inpatient Medical Rehabilitation Facilities* (Tucson, Ariz.: Commission on Accreditation of Rehabilitation Facilities, 1987), 1–19.

9. Elizabeth Nancy Lewis and Patricia Vince Careni, *Nurse Staffing and Patient Classification Strategies for Success* (Rockville, Md.: Aspen Publishers, Inc., 1984), 8.

10. Commission on Accreditation of Rehabilitation Facilities, *Standards Manual for Organizations Serving People with Disabilities* (Tucson, Ariz.: Commission on Accreditation of Rehabilitation Facilities, 1988), 21.

11. Ibid., 22.

12. Elaine M. Lasoff, "Improving Nurses' Cooperation with Clinical Research," *Journal of Nursing Administration* 16, no. 9 (1986): 6.

---

## BIBLIOGRAPHY

Abdellah, Faye G., and Levine, Eugene. *Better Patient Care through Nursing Research.* 2nd ed. New York: Macmillan Publishing Co., Inc., 1980.

Bloch, Doris. "Evaluation of Nursing Care in Terms of Process and Outcome: Issues in Research and Quality Assurance." *Nursing Research* 24 (1975): 256–263.

Bloch, Doris. "Interrelated Issues in Evaluation and Evaluation Research: A Researcher's Perspective." *Nursing Research* 29 (1980): 69–73.

Carey, Raymond G., and Seibert, Jerry H. "Integrating Program Evaluation, Quality Assurance, and Marketing for Inpatient Rehabilitation." *Rehabilitation Nursing* 13 (1988): 66–70.

Conway, M.E. "Clinical Research: Instrument for Change." *Journal of Nursing Administration* 8, no. 12 (1978): 27–32.

Courts, Nancy F. "A Patient Satisfaction Survey for a Rehabilitation Unit." *Rehabilitation Nursing* 13 (1988): 79–81.

Cronewett, Linda R. "Increasing the Cost Effectiveness of Research in Clinical Settings." *Journal of Nursing Administration* 17, no. 5 (1987): 4–5.

Distel, Lori. "More Than Chart Review." *Quality Review Bulletin* 7 (1981): 26–29.

Dunn, Margaret A. "Development of an Instrument To Measure Nursing Performance." *Nursing Research* 19, no. 4 (1970): 502–510.

Ehrat, Karen S. "The Cost-Quality Balance: An Analysis of Quality, Effectiveness, Efficiency, and Cost." *Journal of Nursing Administration* 17, no. 5 (1987): 6–13.

Falvo, Donna R. *Effective Patient Education: A Guide to Increased Compliance.* Rockville, Md.: Aspen Publishers, Inc., 1985.

Ferguson, Ginger H.; Hildman, Tommie; and Nichols, Brenda. "The Effect of Nursing Care Planning Systems on Patient Outcomes." *Journal of Nursing Administration* 17, no. 9 (1987): 30–36.

Gallant, Barbara W., and McLane, Audrey M. "Outcome Criteria: A Process for Validation at the Unit Level." *Journal of Nursing Administration* 9, no. 1 (1979): 14–21.

Gordon, Marjory. "Determining Study Topics." *Nursing Research* 29 (1980): 83–87.

Hamilton, Sharon. "Unit Level Quality Assurance: Essential for Success." *Rehabilitation Nursing* 13 (1988): 76–78.

Hegyvary, S.T., and Haussman, D. "The Relationship of Nursing Process and Patient Outcomes." *Journal of Nursing Administration* 6, no. 9 (1976): 18–21.

Horsley, JoAnne, and Crane, Joyce. U*sing Research To Improve Nursing Practice: A Guide.* New York: Grune & Stratton, 1983.

Hyunok, Do K. "Head Trauma Rehabilitation: Program Evaluation." *Rehabilitation Nursing* 13 (1988): 71–75.

Isaac, Stephen, and Michael, William B. *Handbook in Research and Evaluation.* San Diego, Calif.: EDITS, 1983.

Jackson, Bettie S. "Participant Observation in Nursing Research." *Supervisor Nurse* 4, no. 5 (1973): 30–40.

Kerfoot, K.M., and Watson, C.A. "Research Based Quality Assurance: The Key to Excellence in Nursing." In *Current Issues in Nursing.* 2nd ed., edited by J.C. McCloskey and H.K. Grace. Boston: Blackwell Scientific Publications, 1985, 539–547.

Kibbie, Priscilla. "An Emerging Professional: The Quality Assurance Nurse." *Journal of Nursing Administration* 18, no. 4 (1988): 30–33.

Knox, Alan B., ed. *Assessing the Impact of Continuing Education*, no. 3. San Francisco: Jossey-Bass Inc., Pubs., 1979.

Krueger, Janelle C. "Establishing Priorities for Evaluation and Research: A Nursing Perspective." *Nursing Research* 9, no. 29 (1980): 115–119.

Larson E. "Combining Nursing Quality Assurance and Research Programs." *Journal of Nursing Administration* 8, no. 11 (1983): 32–35.

Lasoff, Elaine M. "Improving Nurses' Cooperation with Clinical Research." *Journal of Nursing Administration* 16, no. 9 (1986): 6–7.

Maciorowski, Linda F.; Larson, Elaine; and Keane, Anne. "Quality Assurance Evaluate Thyself." *Journal of Nursing Administration* 15, no. 6 (1985): 38–42.

Mayer, Marlene G. *A Systematic Approach to the Nursing Care Plan.* New York: Appleton-Century-Crofts, 1977.

Mumley, Mary Jane. "Direct Observation Tool." *AORN Journal* 22 (1975): 191–194.

Phaneuf, Maria C., and Wandelt, Mabel A. "Three Methods of Process-Oriented Nursing Evaluation." *Quality Review Bulletin* 17, no. 8 (1981): 20–26.

Polit, Denise, and Hungler, Bernadette. "Observational Methods." In *Nursing Research Principles and Methods.* Philadelphia: J.B. Lippincott Co., 1983.

Posavac, E.J., and Carey, R.G. "Using a Level of Function Scale (LORS-II) To Evaluate the Success of Inpatient Rehabilitation Programs." *Rehabilitation Nursing* 7 (1982): 17–19.

Puetz, Belinda E., and Peters, Faye L. *Continuing Education for Nurses: A Complete Guide to Effective Programs.* Rockville, Md.: Aspen Publishers, Inc., 1981.

Ramey, Irene G. "Setting Nursing Standards and Evaluating Care." In *Management for Nurses.* 2nd ed., edited by Marie Streng Berger et al. St. Louis: C.V. Mosby Co., 1980, 63–69.

Rizzuto, Carmela, and Mitchell, Malinda. "Research in Service Settings: Part I—Consortium Project Outcomes." *Journal of Nursing Administration* 18, no. 2 (1988): 32–38.

Rizzuto, Carmela, and Mitchell, Malinda. "Research in Service Settings: Part II—Consortium Project." *Journal of Nursing Administration* 18, no. 3 (1988): 19–24.

Tan, Marva West. "Problem Areas in Multidisciplinary Audit." *Quality Review Bulletin* 4 (1978): 33–35.

van Maanen, Hanneke, M.Th. "Improvement of Quality of Nursing Care: A Goal To Challenge in the Eighties." *Journal of Advanced Nursing* 6 (1981): 3–9.

Wandelt, M.A., and Ager, J.A. *Quality Patient Care Scale.* New York: Appleton-Century-Crofts, 1977.

Warner, A. "Education for Roles and Responsibilities in Quality Assurance." *Quality Review Bulletin* 11, no. 3 (1985): 78–80.

Watson, Carol A.; Bulechek, Gloria M.; and McCloskey, Joanne Comi. "QAMUR: A Quality Assurance Model Using Research." *Journal of Nursing Quality Assurance* 2 (1987): 21–27.

Weiss, Carol H. *Evaluation Research: Methods of Assessing Program Effectiveness.* Englewood Cliffs, N.J.: Prentice-Hall, Inc., 1972.

Woody, Mary F. "An Evaluator's Perspective." *Nursing Research* 29 (1980): 74–77.

Young, Delores E., and Ventura, Marlene R. "Application of Nursing Diagnosis in Quality Assessment Research." *Quality Assurance Update* 4, no. 2 (1980): 1–4.

---

## SUGGESTED READINGS

Abdellah, Faye G., and Levine, Eugene. "What Patients Say about Their Nursing Care." *Hospitals* 31, no. 11 (1952): 44–48.

Araujo, Marianne D., and Jurkovic, Joanne T. "The Role of Nursing in Quality Assurance." In *Hospital Quality Assurance, Risk Management and Program Evaluation*, edited by Jesus J. Pena, Alden N. Haffner, Bernard Rosen, and Donald W. Light. Rockville, Md.: Aspen Publishers, Inc., 1984.

Bloch, Doris. "Evaluation of Nursing Care in Terms of Process and Outcome: Issues in Research and Quality Assurance." *Nursing Research* 24, no. 4 (July/August 1975): 256–263.

Bloch, Doris. "Interrelated Issues in Evaluation and Evaluation Research: A Researcher's Perspective." *Nursing Research* 29, no. 2 (March/April 1980): 69–73.

Bruskewitz, Mary A. "Observation As an Evaluation Tool." In *Nursing Quality Assurance: A Unit-Based Approach*, edited by Patricia S. Schroeder and Regina M. Maibusch. Rockville, Md.: Aspen Publishers, Inc., 1984.

Carey, Raymond G., and Seibert, Jerry H. "Integrating Program Evaluation, Quality Assurance, and Marketing for Inpatient Rehabilitation." *Rehabilitation Nursing* 13, no. 2 (1988), 66–70.

Commission on Accreditation of Rehabilitation Facilities. *Standards Manual for Organizations Serving People with Disabilities*. Tucson, Ariz.: Commission on Accreditation of Rehabilitation Facilities, 1988.

Courts, Nancy F. "A Patient Satisfaction Survey for a Rehabilitation Unit." *Rehabilitation Nursing* 13, no. 2 (1988), 79–81.

Coyne, C., and Killien, M. "A System for Unit-Based Monitors of Quality of Nursing Care." *Journal of Nursing Administration* 17, no. 1 (1987): 26–32.

D'Costa, A., and Sechrist, L. *Program Evaluation Concepts for Health Administrators*. Washington: Association of University Programs in Health Administration, 1976.

Deurr, Bonnie L., and Staats, Karen. "Quality Assurance Program Evaluation: A View from the Unit Base." *Journal of Nursing Quality Assurance* 2, no. 4 (1988), 13–16.

DeVincezo, Doris K., and Watkins, Sylvia. "Accidental Falls in a Rehabilitation Setting." *Rehabilitation Nursing* 12, no. 5 (1987), 248–252.

Distel, Lori. "More Than Chart Review." *Quality Review Bulletin* 7, no 7 (1981), 26–29.

Do, Hyunok K.; Sahagian, Debra A.; Schuster, Lois C.; and Sheridan, Susan E. "Head Trauma Rehabilitation: Program Evaluation." *Rehabilitation Nursing* 13, no. 2 (1988), 71–75.

Doering, E.R. "Factors Influencing Inpatient Satisfaction with Care." *Quality Review Bulletin* 9 (1983), 291–299.

Donabedian Avedis. *Explorations in Quality Assessment and Monitoring*. Ann Arbor, Mich.: Health Administration Press, 1980.

Donabedian, Avedis. *The Definition of Quality and Approaches to Its Assessment*. Ann Arbor, Mich.: Health Administration Press, 1980.

Donabedian, Avedis. *Explorations in Quality Assessment and Monitoring, Volume 2: The Criteria and Standards of Quality*. Ann Arbor, Mich.: Health Administration Press, 1982.

Donabedian, Avedis. "Criteria and Standards for Quality Assessment and Monitoring." *Quality*

*Review Bulletin* 12, no. 3 (1986), 99–108.

Driever, Marie J., and Birenbaum, Linda K. "Patton's Utilization—Focused Evaluation as the Basis of the Quality Assurance Process." *Journal of Nursing Quality Assurance* 2, no. 4 (1988), 45–54.

Elbeik, M.A.H. *Developing and Administering a Patient Satisfaction Survey in Health Management.* Chicago: American Hospital Association, 1986.

Falvo, Donna R. "Patient Education As a Process in Patient Care." In *Effective Patient Education: A Guide to Increased Compliance.* Rockville, Md.: Aspen Publishers, Inc., 1985, 31–73.

Fitz-Gibbon, C.T., and Morris, L.L. *How To Design a Program Evaluation.* Beverly Hills, Calif.: Sage, 1978.

Formella, Nancy, and Schroeder, Patricia S. "The Unit-Based System." In *Nursing Quality Assurance: A Unit-Based Approach,* edited by Patricia S. Schroeder and Regina M. Maibusch. Rockville, Md.: Aspen Publishers, Inc., 1984, 29.

Gallant, Barbara W., and McLane, Audrey M. "Outcome Criteria: A Process for Validation at the Unit Level." *Journal of Nursing Administration* 9, no. 1 (1979), 14–21.

Gay, L.R. *Educational Evaluation and Measurement.* Columbus, Ohio: Charles E. Merrill Publishing Co., 1980.

Graham, Nancy O., ed. *Quality Assurance in Hospitals.* Rockville, Md.: Aspen Publishers, Inc., 1982.

Granger, C.V.; Albrecht, G.L.; and Hamilton, B.B. "Outcome of Comprehensive Medical Rehabilitation: Measurement of Pulses, Profile and the Barthel Index." *Archives of Physical Medicine and Rehabilitation* 60 (1979), 145–154.

Greeley, H. *Continuous Monitoring and Data-Based Assessment,* Vols. 1 and 2. Salem, Wisc.: Greeley Associates, Ltd., 1984.

Griffith, J.R. *Measuring Hospital Performance.* Chicago: Inquiry, 1978.

Hamilton, Sharon, and Marales, Barbara J. "Unit-Level Quality Assurance: Essential for Success." *Rehabilitation Nursing* 13, no. 2 (1988), 76–78, 92.

Harmon, Carol A. "Involving Staff in Nursing Quality Assurance." *Quality Review Bulletin* 6, no. 11 (1980), 26–30.

Hegyvary, Sue T. "An Evaluator's Perspective." *Nursing Research* 29 (1980), 91–93.

Hill, Barbara A.; Johnson, Ruth; and Garrett, Betty J. "Reducing the Incidence of Falls in High Risk Patients." *Journal of Nursing Administration* 18, nos. 7 and 8 (July/August 1988), 24–28.

Hinshaw, A.S., and Atwood, J.R. "A Patient Satisfaction Instrument Precision by Replication." *Nursing Research* 31, no. 3 (1982), 170–175.

Holzemer, W.L. "Research and Evaluation: An Overview." *Quality Review Bulletin* 6, no. 3 (March 1980), 31–34.

Horsley, JoAnne, and Crane, Joyce. *Using Research To Improve Nursing Practice: A Guide.* New York: Grune & Stratton, 1983.

Houston, C.S., and Pasanen, W.E. "Patient's Perception of Hospital Care." *Hospitals* 46, no. 4 (1972), 70–74.

Howe, Marilyn. "Developing Instruments for Measurement of Criteria: A Clinical Nursing Practice Perspective." *Nursing Research* 29 (1980), 100–103.

Isaac, Stephen, and Michael, William B. *Handbook in Research and Evaluation.* San Diego: EDITS, 1983.

Joint Commission on Accreditation of Healthcare Organizations. *Monitoring and Evaluation in Nursing Services.* Chicago: Joint Commission on Accreditation of Healthcare Organizations, 1986, 17.

Joint Commission on Accreditation of Healthcare Organizations. *Accreditation Manual for Hospitals/88*. Chicago: Joint Commission on Accreditation of Healthcare Organizations, 1987, 150.

Jones, K.R. "Severity of Illness Measured Systems: An Update." *Nursing Economics* 5 (1987), 292–296.

Kirk, J., and Miller, M.L. *Reliability and Validity in Qualitative Research*. Beverly Hills, Calif.: Sage, 1986.

Krueger, Janelle C. "Establishing Priorities for Evaluation and Evaluation Research: A Nursing Perspective. *Nursing Research* 29, no. 2 (March/April 1980), 115–118.

Lang, Norma M., and Werley, Harriet H. "Evaluation Research: Assessment of Nursing Care." *Nursing Research* 29 (1980), 25–29.

Lindeman, Carol A. "Measuring Quality of Nursing Care: Part One." *Journal of Nursing Administration* 6, no. 6 (1976), 7–9.

Lindeman, Carol A. "Measuring Quality of Nursing Care: Part Two." *Journal of Nursing Administration* 6, no. 7 (1976), 16–19.

Luke, R., and Boss, R.W. "Barriers Limiting the Implementation of Quality Assurance Programs." *Health Services Research* 16 (1981), 305–314.

Lynn, F. "Incidents—Need They Be Accidents?" *American Journal of Nursing* 80, no. 6 (1980), 1098–1101.

Meisenheimer, Claire Gavin, ed. *Quality Assurance: A Complete Guide to Effective Programs*. Rockville, Md.: Aspen Publishers, Inc., 1985.

Meleis, A.I. *Theoretical Nursing: Development and Progress*. Philadelphia: J.B. Lippincott Co., 1985.

Milton, Doris. "Challenges of Quality Assurance Program Evaluation in a Practice Setting." *Journal of Nursing Quality Assurance* 2, no. 4 (1988), 25–34.

Mitchell, K. "Linking Program Evaluation and Quality Assurance." *Journal of Quality Assurance* 7, no. 3 (1985), 8–10.

Morris, L.L., and Fitz-Gibbon, C.T. *How To Measure Program Implementation*. Beverly Hills, Calif.: Sage, 1978.

Patton, M.Q. *Utilization-Focused Evaluation*. Beverly Hills, Calif.: Sage, 1986.

Pena, Jesus J.; Haffner, Alden N.; Rosen, Bernard; and Light, Donald W., eds. *Hospital Quality Assurance, Risk Management, and Program Evaluation*. Rockville, Md.: Aspen Publishers, Inc., 1984.

Phaneuf, Maria C. "Future Direction of Evaluation and Evaluation Research in Health Care: A Nursing Perspective." *Nursing Research* 29, no. 2 (March/April 1980), 123–126.

Phaneuf, Maria C., and Wandelt, Mabel A. "Three Methods of Process-Oriented Nursing Evaluation." *Quality Review Bulletin* 17, no. 8 (1981), 20–26.

Pinkerton, Sue Ellen. "Accountability for Quality Care: Perspectives of a Nurse Administrator." In *Nursing Quality Assurance: A Unit-Based Approach*, edited by Patricia S. Schroeder and Regina M. Maibusch. Rockville, Md.: Aspen Publishers, Inc., 1984.

Pinkerton, Sue Ellen, and Schroeder, Patricia S. *Commitment to Excellence: Developing a Professional Nursing Staff*. Rockville, Md.: Aspen Publishers, Inc., 1988.

Rossi, P.H.; Freeman H.E.; and Wright, S. *Evaluation: A Systematic Approach*. Beverly Hills, Calif., Sage, 1979.

Rowland, Howard S., and Rowland, Beatrice L., eds. "Quality Assurance." In *Nursing Administration Handbook*. 2nd ed. Rockville, Md.: Aspen Publishers, Inc., 1985.

Rowland, Howard S., and Rowland, Beatrice L. *The Manual of Nursing Quality Assurance*, Vol. 1. Rockville, Md.: Aspen Publishers, Inc., 1987.

Saum, Margo F. "Evaluation: A Vital Component of the Quality Assurance Program." *Journal of Nursing Quality Assurance* 2, no. 4 (1988), 17–24.

Schroeder, Patricia S. "The Quality Assurance Process." In *Nursing Quality Assurance: A Unit-Based Approach*, edited by Patricia S. Schroeder and Regina M. Maibusch. Rockville, Md.: Aspen Publishers, Inc., 1984.

Schroeder, Patricia S. "Trends in Quality Assurance: A Vision for the Future." In *Nursing Quality Assurance: A Unit-Based Approach*, edited by Patricia S. Schroeder and Regina M. Maibusch. Rockville, Md.: Aspen Publishers, Inc., 1984.

Schroeder, Patricia S.; Maibusch, Regina M.; Anderson, Cheryl A.; and Formella, Nancy Mansheim. "A Unit-Based Approach to Quality Assurance." *Quality Review Bulletin* 8 (1982), 10–12.

Smeltzer, Carolyn H. "Organizing the Search for Excellence." *Nursing Management* 14, no. 6 (1983), 19–21.

Smeltzer, Carolyn H. "Evaluating Program Effectiveness." In *Quality Assurance: A Complete Guide to Effective Programs*, edited by Claire Gavin Meisenheimer. Rockville, Md.: Aspen Publishers, Inc., 1985, 157–167.

Smeltzer, Carolyn H. "Evaluating a Successful Quality Assurance Program: The Process." *Journal of Nursing Quality Assurance* 2, no. 4 (1988), 1–10.

Smeltzer, Carolyn H.; Feltman, Barbara; and Rajki, Karen. "Nursing Quality Assurance: A Process, Not a Tool." *Journal of Nursing Administration* 13, no. 1 (1983), 5–9.

Vanaguras, Audrone; Egelston, E. Martin; Hopkins, Julie; and Walczak, Regina M. "Principles of Quality Assurance." *Quality Review Bulletin* 5, no. 2 (1979), 3–6.

van Maanen, Hanneke, M. Th. "Improvement of Quality of Nursing Care: A Goal To Challenge in the Eighties." *Journal of Advanced Nursing* 6 (1981), 3–9.

Warner, Kenneth, and Luce, Bryan. *Cost-Benefit and Cost-Effectiveness Analysis in Health Care*. Ann Arbor, Mich.: Health Administration Press, The University of Michigan School of Public Health, 1982.

Watson, C.A.; Bulechek, G.M.; and McCloskey, J.C. "QAMUR: A Quality Assurance Model Using Research." *Journal of Nursing Quality Assurance* 2, no. 1 (November 1987), 21–27.

Weddell, R.; Oddy, M.; and Jenkins, D. "Social Adjustment after Rehabilitation: Two-Year Follow-Up of Patients with Severe Head Injury." *Psychological Medicine* 10 (1980), 257–263.

Wilde, D; Novar, L.; and Isaacs, B. "Facts on Falling." *Health and Social Sciences Journal* 91 (1981), 1413–1415.

Wilson, Cathleen Krueger. "Designing a Quality Assurance Program Evaluation: A Process Model." *Journal of Nursing Quality Assurance* 2, no. 4 (1988), 35–44.

Wilson, Cathleen Krueger. "Program Evaluation: Theory, Method, and Practice." In *Nursing Quality Assurance: A Unit-Based Approach*, edited by Patricia S. Schroeder and Regina M. Maibusch. Rockville, Md.: Aspen Publishers, Inc., 1984.

Wilson, H.S. *Research in Nursing*. Menlo Park, Calif.: Addison-Wesley Publishing Co., Inc., 1985.

Woody, Mary F. "An Evaluator's Perspective." *Nursing Research* 29 (March/April 1980), 74–77.

# Chapter 6

# Rehabilitation Nursing Quality Assurance in the Long-Term Care Setting

## BACKGROUND

Rehabilitation has been defined as a continuous comprehensive team effort to maintain and maximize functioning.[1] The key concept of this definition is the view that rehabilitation is a continuing process and should not be restricted by age or health care setting. However, some health care professionals may believe that older adults are not likely rehabilitation candidates.

The rehabilitation of disabled older adults traditionally has had low priority among rehabilitation professionals.[2] Although the incidence of disabilities increases with age, a recent demographic study indicated that as the incidence of disabilities increases, contact with and service by rehabilitation appear to decrease.[3] A critical quality assurance issue in the long-term care setting is the adequacy of rehabilitation services provided and their use.

It is projected that, by the year 2000, 31 million people in the United States will be 65 years of age and over. Currently, at least one-third of the functionally disabled population is 65 or older.[4] As the country's older population increases, so will the incidence of chronic illnesses and the need for geriatric rehabilitation services, especially in the long-term care setting. The quality of such rehabilitative services must be assessed in terms of the patient who is a short-stay resident (discharge within 90 days or less) in a skilled nursing facility as well as the patient who views the facility as a permanent home.

The emphasis on rehabilitation in the nursing home setting has increased since the introduction of diagnosis-related groups (DRGs). DRGs are part of the health care industry's efforts to provide more efficient and economical health care with an emphasis on decreasing hospital stays. However, the concept of shortening hospital stays has been especially frustrating when caring for elderly patients, who are more frequently hospitalized, have more complicated illnesses, and require longer hospital stays.[5] In order to help resolve the conflict between shortened acute care hospital stays with the delivery of optimal geriatric health care, some hospitals have established closer ties with nursing homes.[6] Many such nursing homes have expanded their rehabilitation services in order to attract short-stay residents. Indeed, nursing homes are now publicizing their rehabilitative services as a marketing tool in order to attract a variety of short-stay patients.

But what of the long-term-stay nursing home residents? Use of rehabilitation could be proven cost-effective by preventing secondary medical complications and quality-effective by maintaining and maximizing function.[7] Research has shown that not only can older adults learn a task and improve with practice but, by giving extensive help with self-care tasks, health care professionals are inducing a "learned helplessness" in disabled older adults.[8] Studies have revealed that older adults improve and benefit from rehabilitation services in such areas as self-care ability, balance, communication, restlessness at night, incontinence, and social skills.[9]

In addition to the "older adult" nursing home residents, long-term care facilities are facing a possible influx of younger patients. Victims of catastrophic injuries such as head injury and spinal cord injury are surviving with extensive functional limitations that prohibit independent living. This fact and the epidemic of acquired immune deficiency syndrome (AIDS) have necessitated that society examine long-term care in a new way. The demand for long-term care for younger patients will increase as the numbers of survivors of catastrophic illness and injuries increase. How will their rehabilitation needs be met? How can quality assurance promote effective long-term patient outcomes?

One major avenue of quality assurance support is found in national consumer organizations such as the National Citizens' Coalition for Nursing Home Reform, as well as in voluntary ombudsman programs and legislative lobbying efforts.[10] A recent survey of over 400 nursing home residents documented answers to the question, "What is quality care?" The most significant component cited was the existence of knowledgeable, highly skilled staff. Clearly, consumer involvement is helping to shape the quality assurance programs of long-term care. Just as certain is the fact that the impact of rehabilitation services will also be a major component of quality assurance monitoring.


## STANDARDS

### Licensure, Certification, and Accreditation

A standard is the measure used to evaluate practice. Minimal standards for licensure, mandated by governmental regulatory bodies, are based on local, state, and federal legislation. Licensure is the mandatory process that permits the legal existence of a long-term care facility. Additionally, certification is required of all facilities involved in the federally funded programs of Medicare and Medicaid.[11]

Voluntary accreditation in long-term care has been developed by the Joint Commission on Accreditation of Healthcare Organizations. Attention is focused on patient/resident care rather than on the functioning of specific departments. Additionally, standards have been added or revised in many areas, including patients' rights, quality of life, rehabilitation care utilization review, and the use of quality assurance findings in competence assessment.[12] Those persons responsible for nursing quality assurance must incorporate both the mandatory and, if needed, voluntary standards into the facility's quality assurance activities.

## Nursing Standards

Most facilities develop their own internal standards. Nursing departments often base such internal measures on professional organizations' standards of practice. Two especially applicable sets of standards for the contemporary long-term care facility are the Standards for Gerontological Nursing Practice and the Standards of Rehabilitation Nursing Practice.

According to the American Nurses' Association, gerontological nursing is:

> concerned with the assessment of the health needs of older adults, planning and implementing health care to meet these needs, and evaluating the effectiveness of such care. Emphasis is placed on maximizing independence in the activities of everyday living and promoting, maintaining, and restoring health.[13]

Quality assurance programs in long-term care facilities should be concerned with measuring patient outcomes as they relate to maximizing independence and promoting quality of life. Part of this process is involving the resident and family in planning care. This is clearly delineated in Standard VI: "The older adult and/ or significant other(s) participate in determining the progress attained in the achievement of established goals."[14]

The concepts expressed throughout the Standards for Gerontological Nursing Practice are closely related to those outlined in the Standards of Rehabilitation Nursing Practice: "The goal of rehabilitation nursing is to assist the individual or group in the restoration and maintenance of maximum physical, psychosocial, and spiritual health."[15] These standards emphasize patient/family involvement in care planning as well as interdisciplinary collaboration. Such collaboration should be part of the nursing quality assurance program in long-term care. Standard VII states:

> The nurse participates in peer review and interdisciplinary program evaluation to assure that high-quality nursing care is provided to individuals in a rehabilitation setting.[16]

These principles apply not only to the older resident, but to the younger patient as well. As younger groups of persons (i.e., victims of head injury, spinal cord injury, AIDS) require long-term care placement, their needs must be incorporated into both nursing and interdisciplinary quality assurance programs. This may require adaptation on the part of staff members who have been used to working with elderly residents only. Patients whose ages span various developmental stages may require a wider variety of interventions than those who formerly were thought of as "typical" geriatric nursing home residents. Nursing quality assurance activities must encompass the entire range of resident needs and expectations.

## ASSESSMENT AND PLANNING

A successful nursing quality assurance program should clearly identify the persons involved and spell out the responsibilities of each. The major purpose of quality assurance is the improvement of patient care. Fulfilling regulatory or accreditation requirements, although important, should not be the primary goal.[17] In order to delineate responsibilities and improve patient care appropriately, the nursing quality assurance committee should review quality assurance needs regularly as they exist in each long-term care facility. A thorough assessment and planning guide was presented in Chapter 3. The following needs assessment and program planning guide is intended to focus on those aspects particularly important to long-term care. A sample nursing quality assurance plan for the long-term care facility is presented in Appendix 6-A.

I.   Assessment.
     A.  *Data collection*. Pertinent data should be collected from the following resources:
         1.  Risk management. The purposes of risk management are to identify and analyze potential risks and to develop measures to reduce or prevent them. As noted in Chapter 3, the following factors are important monitors in rehabilitation as well as in long-term care.
             *a)* Falls. While promoting the concept of independence, long-term care professionals must carefully monitor the risk and occurrence of falls. In addition to the demographic data of residents' diagnosis, age, sex, level of orientation, activity level, and medication routine, two additional factors are of particular importance. Is there a difference in the rate of falls between short- and long-stay residents? This may help to identify differences in care, treatment plan, or rehabilitation services. Also, was the patient physically

restrained at the time of the incident? The use of restraints may
need to be a separate monitoring issue.

b) Use of physical and chemical restraints. The following questions
should be considered: Are restraints used routinely? Have other
interventions been attempted prior to the use of such restraints?
Are there policies to govern the use of physical and chemical
restraints? Do these policies include guidelines for assessment
and nursing documentation? Are the policies followed?

c) Skin integrity. Nursing home residents are often at high risk for
impairment of skin integrity as a result of age, chronic illness, and
mobility difficulties. Monitoring any occurrence of skin breakdown is critical. Equally important is a preventive program to
maintain skin integrity and avoid impairment.

d) Bowel and bladder care. Are residents on programs to promote
independence in bowel and bladder care? Are laxatives and enemas avoided as much as possible? Is the use of indwelling cathe-
ters monitored not only for possible urinary tract infections but
for possible removal and attempts at continence?

e) Medication errors. The monitoring of medication errors is always
important to nursing quality assurance. The rehabilitative aspects
of long-term care support, whenever possible, patient involvement in self-medication programs. As in free-standing rehabilitation facilities, patient error during self-medication regimens must
be incorporated when monitoring medication errors.

2. Utilization review. Utilization review is responsible for evaluating
the use of long-term health care services and facilities against preestablished criteria.

a) Admission criteria. All long-term facilities need admission criteria based on the patient population. Many nursing homes may
need to review criteria in light of the admission of short-stay
residents and younger patients who are the victims of catastrophic
illness and injury. Monitoring admission appropriateness may
help to clarify desired patient outcomes by identifying characteristics of resident populations.

b) Functional status measures. Functional status outcomes, appropriately monitored, will help to clarify program goals and to
measure the success of long-term care.

3. Infection control. Since the majority of nursing home residents are
long-stay patients, the tracking of infections is of critical importance.
Several key monitors include

a) Incidence of urinary tract infections.

b) Incidence of respiratory tract infections.

    *c)* Audits of hand washing before and after providing patient care.

    *d)* Placement of "clean" and "dirty" items in appropriate utility rooms.

  4. Program evaluation. Successful program implementation depends on preestablished, measurable criteria for acceptable patient outcomes. In long-term care, examples of critical program monitors include

    *a)* Interdisciplinary team functioning. The achievement of successful patient outcomes is dependent upon true interdisciplinary team collaboration. All patient programs should be planned by health care professionals and the patient/family as partners in care planning. Utilization of the rehabilitation specialty's concept of team functioning and program evaluation should provide the basis for appropriate program monitors.

    *b)* Patient/family concerns. Patient/family satisfaction should be monitored on a regular basis. Residents may have a length of stay ranging from months to years. During these times, health care consumers have the right to participate in the evaluation of services, and providers have the responsibility to incorporate such input into the plan of care.

  5. Nursing administration. In the long-term care facility, managerial duties may overlap, and nursing administration may oversee a variety of management concerns. The following factors may be part of a comprehensive monitoring system.

    *a)* Patient classification system. Does the acuity system accurately measure nursing care requirements? Does it consider both short- and long-stay residents? Is it flexible enough to allow for the potential needs of a younger group of patients?

    *b)* Staff credentialing. In addition to mandatory licensure, are registered nurses pursuing certification options (e.g., gerontological or rehabilitation nursing certification)? Is there an incentive program to promote certification?

    *c)* Criteria-based job descriptions and performance evaluations. Potential monitors include relevance of performance outcome criteria and methodology of performance evaluations.

    *d)* Nursing documentation. Are there relevant standards for documentation? Are these reviewed and revised annually? Are charts reviewed to measure compliance with charting standards?

    *e)* Patient education. Are patient education programs evaluated as to the success of identified patient outcomes? Do patients/families participate in the evaluation process?

    *f)* Staff development. Are educational requirements part of the nursing department standards? Are programs provided for both professional and nonprofessional nursing staff? Do the programs provide information that is up to date and applicable to the various populations served? Are staff members involved in the presentation of educational material? Are they given the opportunity to attend educational programs outside the facility?

B. *Evaluation of proposed program.* As monitors are established, the usefulness of data should be evaluated on the basis of the following considerations.

  1. The nursing quality assurance program must reflect measurement of the nursing department's standards of practice.

  2. Data must be sufficient in both quantity and quality to measure standard compliance.

  3. The program must measure patient care services as applied to all patient groups (i.e., short-stay, long-stay, AIDS sufferers, and victims of spinal cord or head injury).

  4. The nursing quality assurance program must reflect the facility's mission and philosophy statements as well as those of the nursing department.

  5. The program should provide a means of acknowledging successful nursing outcomes as well as identifying problem areas.

  6. There must be a differentiation between a trend in data and isolated occurrences.

II. Planning.

A. *Purpose.* The purposes of a nursing quality assurance program are to monitor, evaluate, and improve the quality of patient care via a systematic, ongoing process.

B. *Format: Monitor Establishment Form.* Exhibit 6-1 illustrates a sample form for monitor establishment.

  1. Monitor: the specific factor measured that indicates quality of services provided (e.g., the number of patient assessments completed within 48 hours of admission).

  2. Criteria for achievement: the acceptable level of compliance. This may be given in numerical or percentage form.

  3. Data source: the resource providing needed data (e.g., nursing admission assessment form, adverse occurrence reports from risk management).

  4. Data collector: the person(s) responsible for gathering the data to present to the nursing quality assurance committee (e.g., committee chairperson, specific staff nurse).

  5. Reporting frequency: how often data will be reviewed (e.g., monthly, quarterly).

**Exhibit 6-1** Monitor Establishment Form

| Monitor | Criteria for Achievement | Data Source | Data Collector | Reporting Frequency |
|---|---|---|---|---|
|  |  |  |  |  |

C. *Format: Monitor Reporting Form.* After monitors have been established, criteria have been identified, and methodology has been organized (Exhibit 6-1), a reporting format must be developed. A sample reporting form is illustrated in Exhibit 6-2. The monitor and criteria columns are identical with those in the Monitor Establishment Form. The differences in the Monitor Reporting Form are as follows:
   1. Results: the results of data collection. These may be reported in numerical or percentage form, whichever way has been established in the criteria.
   2. Analysis: whether or not the criteria have been achieved.
   3. Action: action and/or recommendations identified by the committee to improve or maintain care, based on the analysis.

## Committee Membership

The final step prior to implementation is establishing committee membership. The chairperson of the nursing quality assurance committee should hold a managerial position and ensure that quality assurance activities are discussed with the entire nursing administration team. This should facilitate actions to improve care and identify both actual and potential problems. Members should include at least one other nurse manager, representatives from all shifts, and representatives from all levels of the nursing staff, including unlicensed personnel. Results of committee activities should be shared with the staff members so that they are involved in the planning, implementation, and evaluation of the services they provide.

## IMPLEMENTATION

The implementation process is based on the foundation developed during the assessment and planning stages. A critical step in the implementation process is the structure of committee meetings. A successful meeting usually signals successful implementation.

## Committee Meeting Format

The following guidelines are meant to help the nursing quality assurance chairperson conduct an efficient meeting. Meetings should be conducted at least monthly.

Exhibit 6-2 Monitor Reporting Form

| Monitor | Criteria | Results | Analysis | Action |
|---------|----------|---------|----------|--------|
|         |          |         |          |        |

1. Review of minutes. Minutes of the preceding meeting should be carefully reviewed and corrected as necessary. This helps to ensure accuracy and record progress made in enhancing patient care services.
2. Old business. A review of old business offers a time for completing unfinished reports, finalizing review results, or clarifying unfinished or unclear responsibilities. Reviewing unfinished business and documenting progress toward resolution help to ensure that projects and problems are resolved and appropriate action taken.
3. Reports. A regular time slot for review and discussion of monitor reporting and reviewing study results should be established.
4. New business. This time should be utilized for establishment of new monitors, discussion of recommendations from the staff of various patient care areas, and discussion of interdisciplinary concerns as well.

### Monitor Implementation

The actual monitoring is the result of a well-planned, systematic method of data collection. Table 6-1 offers examples of established monitors, and Table 6-2 illustrates reporting based on data collection.

Equally important in monitoring implementation is the impact of interdisciplinary monitoring. Table 6-3 illustrates a program quality assurance report that should be reviewed, and nursing's role that should be analyzed during nursing quality assurance meetings.

Monitor implementation is linked to the evaluation process. It is not possible to separate completely these two facets of quality assurance activities. Analysis of data collection begins with differentiating between the concepts of patterns and trends.

## EVALUATION

### Patterns versus Trends

A pattern in quality assurance data means that various outcomes of patient care are characteristic of a particular facility's nursing care. These outcomes allow for minimal variability within an established range based on departmental standards. A trend in quality assurance is a result or results of data collection that fall outside the established range of acceptance. Trends are either widely outside the range, occurring as an isolated problem, or a steadily widening gap between acceptable and unacceptable standards. Trends are the indicators of problems or potential problems.

**Table 6-1** Nursing Quality Assurance Monitors

| Monitor | Criterion | Data Source | Data Collector | Reporting Frequency |
|---|---|---|---|---|
| Number of medication errors per month | Less than 4 | Adverse occurrence reports | Committee chairperson | Monthly |
| Percentage of nursing admission assessments completed within 48 hours of admission | 100% | Patient charts | Head nurses | Quarterly |
| Percentage of monthly weights recorded | 100% | Patient charts | Staff nurses | Monthly |
| Percentage of charts containing patient/family goal documentation within five days of admission | 100% | Patient charts | Head nurses | Quarterly |

**Table 6-2** Monitor Reporting Form (Reporting Period January–March 1988)

| Monitor | Criterion | Results | Analysis | Action |
|---|---|---|---|---|
| Number of medication errors per month | Less than 4 | January, 3<br>February, 3<br>March, 2 | Criterion met | Continue monitoring |
| Number of monthly weights recorded | 100% | January, 100%<br>February, 100%<br>March, 100% | Criterion met | Continue monitoring |
| Percentage of nursing admission assessments completed within 48 hours of admission | 100% | January, 100%<br>February, 100%<br>March, 98% | Criterion met<br>Criterion met<br>Criterion not met | Continue monitoring<br>Continue monitoring<br>1. Review chart<br>2. Assess staffing influences<br>3. Identify cause |

**Table 6-3** Program Monitor Reporting Form (Reporting Period January–March 1988)

| Monitor | Criterion | Results | Analysis | Action |
|---|---|---|---|---|
| Percentage of patients who maintained or improved in mobility status | 60% | January, 65% February 68% March, 68% | Criterion achieved | Continue monitoring |
| Percentage of patients participating in monthly community outings | 70% | January, 70% February, 70% March, 74% | Criterion achieved | Continue monitoring |
| Percentage of patients who maintain or improve in self-care activities | 60% | January, 60% February, 62% March, 62% | Criterion achieved | Continue monitoring |

**Table 6-4** Trend in Nursing Quality Assurance Data

| Monitor | Criterion | Results | Analysis | Action |
|---|---|---|---|---|
| Percentage of nursing admission assessments completed within 48 hours of admission | 100% | January, 100% February 94% March, 88% | January, criterion met February, criterion not met March, criterion not met | January, continue monitoring February/March 1. Identify unit compliance 2. Review admission data 3. Review staffing |

**Analyzing Results**

Table 6-4 illustrates a trend in nursing quality assurance data over a three-month period. The criterion for nursing admission assessment completion was not met, by increasing increments, in February and March.

The nursing quality assurance committee developed the following action plan for evaluation and problem resolution.

- Each nursing unit's individual record of criterion achievement would be examined. This should identify whether the problem was department-wide or confined to a particular unit.
- After establishing the primary location(s) of the problem, the charts of the patients admitted during February and March would be reviewed for the following factors.
    1. admission dates, times, and day of week
    2. patients' diagnoses, estimated lengths of stay, orientation status, and acuity
    3. medical complications, including emergency transfer to acute care hospitals, that took place during the first 48 hours after admission

    These factors might identify changes in acuity that hamper the normal admission process.
- Staffing on the days of admission would be reviewed for:
    1. appropriateness of the staff/patient ratio based on the patient classification system
    2. staff familiarity with admission procedures (e.g., new staff, float staff, etc.)

Once this review was finished, the nursing quality assurance committee would make final recommendations. These could include

- reallocation of staff
- education regarding assessments
- staff counseling

This particular monitor would be carefully checked throughout the next several months to assess progress toward problem resolution. The key to the success of any quality assurance program is its impact on problem resolution toward improving patient care.

## SUMMARY

The long-term care facility is undergoing a variety of changes. An increasing emphasis on rehabilitation services and all changes in patient populations must be addressed in the nursing quality assurance program. The need for interdisciplinary collaboration is at an all-time high. Those persons responsible for directing and coordinating nursing quality assurance activities must incorporate measurements to assess the impact of these recent changes on nursing practice. They must also involve all levels of staff in the understanding and support of long-term-care quality assurance needs.

### NOTES

1. G. Clark and B. Bray, "Development of a Rehabilitation Plan," in *Rehabilitation in the Aging*, ed. T.F. Williams (New York: Raven Press, 1984), 125–143.

2. F. Steinberg, "Education in Geriatrics in Physical Medicine Residency Training Programs, " *Archives of Physical Medicine and Rehabilitation* 65 (1984): 8–10.

3. R. Blake, "Disabled Older Persons: A Demographic Analysis, " *Journal of Rehabilitation* (October/November/December 1981): 19–27.

4. S. Bonstelle and A. Govoni, "Into Aging: Exploring Aging through Games," *Rehabilitation Nursing* (March/April 1984): 23–27.

5. Donald D. Tresch et al., "Coping with Diagnosis Related Groups—The Changing Role of the Nursing Home," *Archives of Internal Medicine* 148 (1988): 1393.

6. Ibid.

7. Rochelle M. Carlson, "Adult Rehabilitation Attitudes and Implications," *Journal of Gerontological Nursing* 14, no. 2 (February 1988): 24–30.

8. J. Avorn and E. Langer, "Induced Disability in Nursing Home Patients: A Controlled Trial," *Journal of the American Geriatrics Society* 30 (1982): 397–400.

9. M.F. Jackson, "Geriatric Rehabilitation on an Acute-Care Medical Unit," *Journal of Advanced Nursing* 9 (1984): 441–448.

10. National Citizens' Coalition for Nursing Home Reform, *A Consumer Perspective on Quality Care: The Residents' Point of View* (Washington: National Citizens' Coalition for Nursing Home Reform, April 1985).

11. Margaret Ross Kraft, Janice Ann Neubauer, and Joan LeSage, "Quality Monitoring in Long-Term Care," *Journal of Nursing Quality Assurance* 2 (1987): 39–48.

12. Joint Commission on Accreditation of Healthcare Organizations, *Long Term Care Standards Manual* (Chicago: Joint Commission on Accreditation of Healthcare Organizations, 1988).

13. American Nurses' Association, *Standards of Gerontological Nursing Practice* (Kansas City, Mo.: American Nurses' Association, 1976), 3.

14. Ibid., 7.

15. American Nurses' Association and Association of Rehabilitation Nurses, *Standards of Rehabilitation Nursing Practice* (Kansas City, Mo.: American Nurses' Association, 1986), 2.

16. Ibid., 11.

17. Mary Ann Lowe and John A. Lowe, *Quality Assurance in Long-Term Care Facilities*, 3rd ed. (Ann Arbor, Mich.: Commission on Professional and Hospital Activities, 1988), 1–10.

## BIBLIOGRAPHY

Abdellah, Faye G. "Nursing Care of the Aged in the United States." *Journal of Gerontological Nursing* 7 (1981): 657–663.

Abdellah, Faye G., and Levine, Eugene. *Better Patient Care through Nursing Research.* 2nd ed. New York: Macmillan Publishing Co., Inc., 1980.

Aiken, L.H., et al. "Teaching Nursing Homes: Prospects for Improving Long-Term Care." *Journal of the American Geriatrics Society* 33 (1985): 196–201.

American Nurses' Association. *Standards of Generic Nursing Practice.* Kansas City, Mo.: American Nurses' Association, 1973.

American Nurses' Association. *Standards of Gerontological Nursing Practice.* Kansas City, Mo.: American Nurses' Association, 1976.

American Nurses' Association. *A Challenge for Change: The Role of Gerontological Nursing.* Kansas City, Mo.: American Nurses' Association, 1982.

Andrews, K.; Brocklehurst, J.C.; Richards, B.; and Laycok, P.J. "The Influence of Age on the Clinical Presentation and Outcome of Stroke." *International Rehabilitation Medicine* 6 (1984): 49–53.

Avorn, J., and Langer, E. "Induced Disability in Nursing Home Patients: A Controlled Trial." *Journal of the American Geriatrics Society* 30 (1982): 397–400.

Benson, E.R., and McDevitt, J.Q. "Health Promotion by Nursing Care of the Elderly." *Nursing and Health Care* 3 (1982): 39–43.

Bloch, Doris. "Evaluation of Nursing Care in Terms of Process and Outcome: Issues in Research and Quality Assurance." *Nursing Research* 24 (1975): 256.

Bowe, J. "Measuring Quality of Care." *Today's Nursing Home* 8, no. 4 (1987): 1.

Brower, H. Terri. "Editorial-Determinants of Quality Nursing Care." *Journal of Gerontological Nursing* 14, no. 2 (February 1988): 7, 41.

Cameron, J.M. "Case Mix and Resource Use in Long Term Care." *Med Care* 23 (1985): 297.

Canar, Mary Jo, and Johnson, Joseph C. "An Employee Learning Needs Assessment Concerning Mental Health Needs of Residents in a Long-Term Care Setting." *Journal of Continuing Education in Nursing* 17 (1986): 5–11.

Cantor, Marjorie Moore. *Achieving Nursing Care Standards: Internal and External.* Rockville, Md.: Aspen Publishers, Inc., 1978.

Carlson, Rochelle M. "Adult Rehabilitation Attitudes and Implications." *Journal of Gerontological Nursing* 14, no. 2 (February 1988): 27–29.

Chavasse, Judith. "From Task Assignment to Patient Allocation: A Change Evaluation." *Journal Advanced Nursing* 6 (1981): 137–145.

Chow, R.K. "Quality of Care: A Present and Future Challenge for All Nurses." *Journal of Gerontological Nursing* 6 (1980): 256–259.

Clark, G., and Bray, B. "Development of a Rehabilitation Plan." In *Rehabilitation in the Aging,* Edited by T.F. Williams. New York: Raven Press, 1984, 125–143.

Clough, Dorothy H., and Derdiarian, Anayis, "A Behavioral Checklist To Measure Dependence and Independence." *Nursing Research* 24, no. 1 (January–February 1980): 55–58.

Committee on Nursing Home Regulation. *Improving the Quality of Care in Nursing Homes.* Washington: Institute of Medicine, National Academy Press, 1986.

Davis, Barbara A., and Lee, Patricia L. "Standards of Gerontological/Long Term Care Nursing Practice." *Quality Review Bulletin* 13 (1987): 377–379.

Donabedian, Avedis. *The Definition of Quality and Approaches to Its Assessment*, Vol 1. Ann Arbor, Mich.: Health Administration Press, 1980.

Eggert, G.M.; Granger, C.V.; Morris, R.; and Pendleton, S.F. "Caring for the Patient with Long-Term Care Disability." *Geriatrics* 32 (1977): 102–114.

Eliopoulos, C. "A Self Care Model for Gerontological Nursing." *Geriatric Nursing* 5 (1984): 366–368.

Ford, B. "Rehabilitation of the Elderly." *Medical Journal of Australia* 1 (1981): 392–396.

Gamroth, Sister Lucia. "Long Term Care Resource Requirements before and after the Prospective Payment System." *IMAGE: Journal of Nursing Scholarship* 20 (1988): 7–11.

Gordon, Marjory. "Determining Study Topics." *Nursing Research* 29 (1980): 83–87.

Gottlieb, T.W. "Quality Assurance in a Long-Term Care Facility." *Quality Review Bulletin* 10 (1984): 51-54.

Gregor, Sara; McCarthy, Kathleen; Chivirchak, Diane; Meluch, Maryann; and Mion, Lorraine C. "Characteristics and Functional Outcomes of Elderly Rehabilitation Patients." *Rehabilitation Nursing* 11, no. 3 (1986): 10–14.

Hall, Geri Richards. "Alterations in Thought Process." *Journal of Gerontological Nursing* 14, no. 3 (March 1988): 30–37.

Harel, Z. "Quality of Care, Congruence, and Well-Being among Institutionalized Aged." *Gerontologist* 21 (1981): 523–531.

Harmon, Carol A. "Involving Staff in Nursing Quality Assurance." *Quality Review Bulletin* 6, no. 11 (1980): 26–30.

Harron, J., and Schaeffer, J. "DRG's and Long Term Care." *Geriatric Nursing* 7 (1986): 31–33.

Hart, Monica A. "Quality Assurance Programs in the Long-Term Care Facility." In *Quality Assurance: A Complete Guide to Effective Programs*, edited by Claire Gavin Meisenheimer. Rockville, Md.: Aspen Publishers, Inc., 1985, 279–293.

Hegyvary, Sue T. "An Evaluator's Perspective." *Nursing Research* 29 (1980): 25–29.

Heller, B.R.; Bausell, R.B.; and Nemos, M. "Nurses' Perceptions of Rehabilitation Potential of Institutionalized Aged." *Journal of Gerontological Nursing* 10, no. 7 (1984): 22–27.

Hewitt, S.M., et al. "Process Auditing in Long-Term Care Facilities." *Quality Review Bulletin* 11 (1985): 6–15.

Hiatt, L.G. "The Environment As a Participant in Health Care." *Journal of Long-Term Care Administration* 10 (1982): 1–17.

Horsley, Joanne, and Crane, Joyce. *Using Research To Improve Nursing Practice: A Guide*. New York: Grune & Stratton, 1983.

Huey, F.L. "What Teaching Nursing Homes Are Teaching Us." *American Journal of Nursing* 85 (1985): 678–83.

Jelinek, R.C., et al. *A Methodology for Monitoring Quality of Nursing Care* (DHEW Publication No. (HRA) 76-25). Washington: U.S. Government Printing Office, 1974.

Joint Commission on Accreditation of Healthcare Organizations. *Long Term Care Standards Manual*. Chicago: Joint Commission on Accreditation of Healthcare Organizations, 1988.

Knowles, Malcolm. *The Modern Practice of Adult Education*. Chicago: Follett Publishing Co., 1980.

Knowles, Malcolm. *The Adult Learner: A Neglected Species*. Houston: Gulf Publishing Co., 1984.

Kraft, Margaret Ross; Neubauer, Janice Ann; and LeSage, Joan. "Quality Monitoring in Long-Term Care." *Journal of Nursing Quality Assurance* 2 (1987): 39–48.

Langford, Teddy. "The Evaluation of Nursing: Necessary and Possible." *Supervisor Nurse* 2, no. 11 (1971): 65–75.

Lawlor, A. "Reader Roundup: Sicker Patients Trigger Staff Alterations." *Today's Nursing Home* 5 (1984): 41–42.

Lindy, Cheryl N. "A Three-Part Approach to Quality Assurance in Nursing." *Quality Review Bulletin* 6 (1980): 12–16.

Linn, M.W., and Linn, B.S. "Qualities of Institutional Care That Affect Outcome." *Aged Care and Services Review* 2 (1980): 1–14.

Lowe, Mary Ann. "What Do We Say? How Do We Say It?" In *Patient Care Plans in Long-Term Care Facilities*. Mobridge, S.D.: Nursing Home Publishing Associates, 1986.

Lowe, Mary Ann, and Lowe, John A. *Quality Assurance in Long-Term Care Facilities*. 3rd ed. Ann Arbor, Mich.: Commission on Professional and Hospital Activities, 1988.

Mason, Elizabeth. *How To Write Meaningful Nursing Standards*. New York: John Wiley & Sons, Inc., 1978.

Mayer, Marlene G.; Norby, Ronald B.; and Watson, Annita B. *Quality Assurance for Patient Care: Nursing Perspectives*. New York: Appleton-Century-Crofts, 1977.

Micheletti, Julie A., and Shlala, Thomas J. "RUGS II: Implications for Management and Quality in Long Term Care." *Quality Review Bulletin* 12 (1986): 236–242.

Millard, P.H., and Smith, C.S. "Personal Belongings—A Positive Effect." *Gerontologist* 21 (1981): 85–90.

Miller, Sister Patricia, and Russel, Dorothy A. "Elements Promoting Satisfaction." *Journal of Gerontological Nursing* 6 (1980): 121–129.

Morgan, D. "Nurses' Perceptions of Mental Confusion in the Elderly: Influence of Resident and Setting Characteristics." *Journal of Health and Social Sciences* 26 (1985): 102–112.

National Citizens' Coalition for Nursing Home Reform. *A Consumer Perspective on Quality Care: The Residents' Point of View*. Washington: National Citizens' Coalition for Nursing Home Reform, April 1985.

Neugarten, Bernice L.; Havighurst, Robert J.; and Tobin, Sheldon S. "The Measurement of Life Satisfaction." *Journal of Gerontology* 16 (April 1961): 134–143.

O'Brien C. "Adult Day Health Care and the Bottom Line." *Geriatric Nursing* 2 (1981): 283–286.

O'Donnell, J.F.; Hannan, E.L.; and Leskowich, W.K. "The Restructuring and Evaluation of the Patient Medical Review in New York State." *Journal of Long-Term Care Administration* 12 (1984): 10–18.

Panicucci, C.L. "Functional Assessment of the Older Adult in the Acute Care Setting." *Nursing Clinics of North America* 18 (1983): 355–362.

Penn, Cathy. "Promoting Independence." *Journal of Gerontological Nursing* 14, no. 3 (March 1988): 14–19.

Phaneuf, Maria C., and Wandelt, Mabel A. "Obstacles to and Potentials for Nursing Quality Appraisal." *Quality Review Bulletin* 7 (1981): 2–5.

Poe, Stephanie Storto, and Will, Janet Carney. "Quality Nurse-Patient Outcomes: A Framework for Nursing Practice." *Journal of Nursing Quality Assurance* 2 (1987): 29–37.

Rankin, N., and Burggraf, V. "Aging in the 80's." *Journal of Gerontological Nursing* 9 (1983): 272–275.

Rosendahl, P.P., and Ross, V. "Does Your Behavior Affect Your Patient's Response?" *Journal of*

*Gerontological Nursing* 8 (1982): 572–575.

Schmied, Elsie. "Living with Cost Containment." *Journal of Nursing Administration* 10 (1980): 1147.

Silverstone, Barbara, and Hyman, Helen Kandel. *You & Your Aging Parent.* New York: Pantheon Books, 1976.

Simmons, V.; Fittipaldi, L.: Holovet, E.; Mones, P.; Gerardi, R.; and Mech, A. "Assessing the Quality of Care in Skilled Nursing Homes." *Journal of Long-Term Care Administration* 9 (1981): 1–17.

Sniff, David. "The Evolution of a Quality Assurance Program." *Quality Review Bulletin* 6 (1980): 26–29.

Somers, A.R. "Long-Term Care for the Elderly and Disabled." *New England Journal of Medicine* 307 (1982): 221–226.

Steiger, N.J., and Lipson, J.G. *Self-Care Nursing: Theory and Practice.* Bowie, Md.: Prentice-Hall, Inc., 1985.

Travis, Shirley S., and McAuley, William J. "Medicaid Elders in a Rehabilitation Trajectory." *Rehabilitation Nursing* 12 (1987): 77–81.

Vetter, Norman. "Performance Indicators in the Care of the Elderly." *Nursing Times* (April 1, 1987): 30–32.

Waters, Gloria. "Determining Criteria Responsibility." *Hospital Peer Review* 3 (1978): 51.

Winn, S., and McCaffree, K.M. "Characteristics of the Nursing Home Perceived Efficient." *Gerontologist* 16 (1976): 415–419

Woody, Mary F. "An Evaluator's Perspective." *Nursing Research* 29 (1980): 74–77.

Yurick, Ann Gera; Spier, Barbara Elliott; Rob, Susanne S.; and Ebert, Nancy J. *The Aged Person and the Nursing Process.* 2nd ed. Norwalk, Conn.: Appelton-Century-Crofts, 1984.

## SUGGESTED READINGS

Abdellah, Faye G.; Beland, Irene L.; Almeda, Martin; and Matheney, Ruth V. *Patient Centered Approaches to Writing.* New York: Macmillan Publishing Co., Inc., 1960.

Acton, N. "The World's Response to Disability: Evolution of a Philosophy." *Archives of Physical Medicine and Rehabilitation* 63 (1982): 145–149.

Aitken, M.J. "Self-Concept and Functionalized Independence in the Hospitalized Elderly." *American Journal of Occupational Therapy* 36 (1982): 243–250.

Black, Mary K. "The Consumer: Product of Our Efforts." In *Quality Assurance: A Complete Guide to Effective Programs,* edited by Claire Gavin Meisenheimer. Rockville, Md.: Aspen Publishers, Inc., 1985.

Brown, M. *Readings in Gerontology.* 2nd ed. St. Louis: C.V. Mosby Co., 1978.

Bull, Margaret J. "Quality Assurance: Its Origins, Transformations, and Prospects." In *Quality Assurance: A Complete Guide to Effective Programs,* edited by Claire Gavin Meisenheimer. Rockville, Md.: Aspen Publishers, Inc., 1985.

Dobson, C.; Powers, E.A.; Keith, P.N.; and Willis, J.G. "Anomia, Self-Esteem, and Life Satisfaction: Interrelationships among Three Scales of Well-Being." *Journal of Gerontology* 14 (1979): 569–572.

Donabedian, Avedis. *The Definition of Quality and Approaches to Its Assessment.* Ann Arbor, Mich.: Health Administration Press, 1980.

Gallant, Barbara W., and McLane, Audrey M. "Outcome Criteria: A Process for Validation at the Unit Level." *Journal of Nursing Administration* 9, no. 1 (1979): 14–21.

Goldfarb, A.I. "Depression in the Old and Aged." In *The Nature and Treatment of Depression*, edited by F. Flatch and S. Draghi. New York: John Wiley & Sons, Inc., 1975.

Gordon, Marjory. "Determining Study Topics." *Nursing Research* 29 (1980): 83–87.

Hart, Monica A. "Quality Assurance Programs in the Long-Term Care Facility." In *Quality Assurance: A Complete Guide to Effective Programs*, edited by Claire Gavin Meisenheimer. Rockville, Md.: Aspen Publishers, Inc., 1985.

Horn, Barbara J. "Establishing Valid and Reliable Criteria: A Researcher's Perspective." *Nursing Research* 29 (1980): 88–90.

Krueger, Janelle C. "Establishing Priorities for Evaluation and Evaluation Research: A Nursing Perspective." *Nursing Research* 9, no. 29(1980): 115–118.

Kulpa, Judith. "Interdisciplinary Review in Long-Term Care." *Quality Review Bulletin* 4 (1978): 15–21.

Lang, Norma M. "Evaluating Health and Nursing Care." *Quality Assurance Update* 111 (1979): 1–6.

Lawton, M.P., and Brody, E. "Assessment of Older People: Self-Maintaining and Instrumental Activities of Daily Living." *Gerontologist* 9 (1969): 179–185.

Lowe, Mary Ann, and Lowe, John A. *Quality Assurance in Long Term Care Facilities.* Ann Arbor, Mich.: Commission on Professional and Hospital Activities, 1988.

Maslow, A.H. *Motivation and Personality.* New York: Harper & Row, 1970.

Meisenheimer, Claire Gavin, ed. *Quality Assurance: A Complete Guide to Effective Programs.* Rockville, Md.: Aspen Publishers, Inc., 1985.

Moore, Karen R. "Nurses Learn from Nursing Audit." *Nursing Outlook* 27 (1979): 254–258.

Moore, Karen R. "Quality Assurance and Nursing Audit: Are They Effective?" *Nursing Management* 13 (1982): 18–22.

Orem, Dorthea E. *Nursing: Concepts of Practice.* St. Louis, Mo.: McGraw-Hill Book Co., 1971.

Pena, Jesus J.; Haffner, Alden N.; Rosen, Bernard; and Light, Donald W., eds. *Hospital Quality Assurance Risk Management and Program Evaluation.* Rockville, Md.: Aspen Publishers, Inc., 1984.

Phaneuf, Maria C. "Future Direction of Evaluation and Evaluation Research in Health Care: A Nursing Perspective." *Nursing Research* 29, no. 2 (1980): 123–126.

Posner, James R. "Insurance and Health Care Cost Containment." In *Hospital Quality Assurance Risk Management and Program Evaluation*, edited by Jesus J. Pena, Alden N. Haffner, Bernard Rosen, and Donald W. Light. Rockville, Md.: Aspen Publishers, Inc., 1984.

Roy, Sister Callista. *Introduction to Nursing: An Adaptation Model.* Englewood Cliffs, N.J.: Prentice-Hall, Inc., 1976.

Schroeder, Patricia S., and Maibusch, Regina M., eds. *Nursing Quality Assurance: A Unit-Based Approach.* Rockville, Md.: Aspen Publishers, Inc., 1984.

Schroeder, Patricia S.; Maibusch, Regina M.; Anderson, Cheryl A.; and Formella, Nancy Mansheim. "A Unit Based Approach to Quality Assurance." *Quality Review Bulletin* 8 (1982): 10–12.

Susset, V., and Vobecky, J. "Disability Outcome and Self-Assessment of Disabled Persons: An Analysis of 506 Cases." *Archives of Physical Medicine and Rehabilitation* 60 (1979): 50–56.

Ventura, Marlene; Hageman, Paul T.; Slakter, Malcolm J.; and Fox, Richard N. "Interrater Reliabilities for Two Measures of Nursing Care Quality." *Research in Nursing and Health* 3 (1980): 25–32.

Watson, Annita, and Mayers, Marlene. "Evaluating the Quality of Patient Care through Retrospective Chart Review." *Journal of Nursing Administration* 6, no. 3 (1976): 17–21.

Woody, Mary F. "An Evaluator's Perspective." *Nursing Research* 29 (1980): 74–77.

Young, Delores E., and Ventura, Marlene R. "Application of Nursing Diagnosis in Quality Assessment Research." *Quality Assurance Update* 4, no. 2 (1980): 1–4.

Zimmer, Marie J. "A Model for Evaluating Nursing Care." *Hospitals* 48 (1974): 91–95, 131.

Zimmer, Marie J., guest ed. "Quality Assurance." *Nursing Clinics of North America* 9 (1974).

# Appendix 6-A

# Sample Nursing Quality Assurance Plan for a Long-Term Care Facility

## INTRODUCTION

The department of nursing of _____, a long-term care facility, is dedicated to providing patient care that is appropriate in quality. The department believes that patient care effectiveness can best be measured by an ongoing, systematic program that is consistent with the mission, philosophy, standards, and goals of both the department of nursing and the facility.

## PURPOSE

The purpose of the quality assurance plan is to maintain and/or improve the appropriateness and quality of nursing practice via a systematic, ongoing plan of monitoring and evaluation of specific aspects of care.

## PROGRAM OBJECTIVES

- To evaluate nursing practice by establishing monitors and criteria, based on departmental standards, for the analysis of patient care
- to identify trends, potential problems, and actual problems in nursing practice
- to monitor the appropriateness, timeliness, and effectiveness of problem resolution
- to involve all levels of nursing personnel in the identification and resolution of problems that impact on nursing practice

## PROGRAM ACCOUNTABILITY

The director of nursing retains final authority and accountability for the implementation of nursing quality assurance activities. A designated committee chairperson is responsible for coordinating the nursing quality assurance program. She or he is the nursing department representative to the facility-wide quality assurance committee. The chairperson is responsible for communicating program findings to the nursing administrative team and ensuring that quality assurance information is relayed to nursing staff. In addition to the chairperson, committee membership includes the head nurses, the staff development director, and staff representatives from all three shifts. At least one representative from all levels of the nursing staff sit on the committee. The nursing quality assurance committee meets on a monthly basis.

## COMMITTEE RESPONSIBILITIES

- Identify and/or review, on an annual basis, nursing department standards that describe the desired level of nursing practice.
- Establish monitors for the evaluation of nursing practice.
- Establish objective, standard-based criteria by which to measure patient care effectiveness.
- Collect and analyze relevant data to determine strengths, weaknesses, and potential problems in nursing practice.
- Recommend actions to maintain and/or improve nursing care.
- Assess the effectiveness of actions taken to resolve problems and improve care.
- Document all committee activities and committee meeting minutes.
- Review and revise the nursing quality assurance program on an annual basis.
- Integrate nursing quality assurance activities with those of the facility-wide quality assurance program.
- Develop quarterly reports and present them to the facility quality assurance committee.

## PROGRAM DESCRIPTION

- The identification of potential and actual problems is formulated by comparing actual nursing practice to nursing department standards.
- Monitors are established utilizing structure, process, and outcome standards.
- Criteria for acceptable level of practice are identified for each monitor.
- Sources of data, the person(s) responsible for collecting data, and reporting frequency are established (Exhibit 6-A-1).

**Exhibit 6-A-1** Monitor Form

| Monitor | Outcome Criteria | Data Source | Responsible Person(s) | Frequency |
|---------|------------------|-------------|-----------------------|-----------|
|         |                  |             |                       |           |

- Specific sources of data collection include but are not limited to
    1. nursing documentation
    2. adverse occurrence reports
    3. problem identification forms
    4. patient satisfaction surveys
    5. physician/staff concerns
    6. communication from facility committees:
        (a) infection control
        (b) risk management
        (c) quality assurance
        (d) utilization management
        (e) medical records
        (f) safety
        (g) medical executive
        (h) pharmacy and therapeutics
        (i) unit staff meetings
        (j) nursing administration meetings
        (k) case management
    7. evaluation of both staff development and patient education programs
    8. results of surveys by outside organizations
    9. patient acuity
    10. patient classification system
    11. performance evaluations
- Monitoring results will be reported to the director of nursing and head nurses. Information that impacts on nursing practice will be shared with the nursing staff.
- Identified problems are resolved at the lowest level possible. Priority for problem solving is based on considering problems that
    1. result in delays in patient care
    2. alter patient care effectiveness
    3. impact on program outcomes
    4. influence interdisciplinary collaboration
- The nursing quality assurance committee recommends action for problem resolution based on evaluation of collected data. Resolution of problems may be achieved by
    1. educational programs
    2. altering existing resources (supplies, staffing patterns, etc.)

**Exhibit 6-A-2** Monitor Report Form

Report Period _____

| Monitor | Criteria | Findings | Analysis | Action |
|---------|----------|----------|----------|--------|
|         |          |          |          |        |

3. reassessment of standards, goals, and objectives

4. personnel counseling

- The corrective action should address the cause of the problem. The action plan should identify the expected outcome, who is responsible for effecting the change, the appropriate action, and the anticipated time frame for resolution. Exhibit 6-A-2 is the Monitor Report Form that identifies evaluative action.

- The director of nursing maintains responsibility for problem resolution and evaluating effectiveness of action.

- All nursing personnel are responsible for the delivery of quality nursing care. Thus, they are also responsible for problem identification and resolution. Effective patient outcomes, including interdisciplinary program actions, are the ultimate responsibility of all personnel.

- The effectiveness of problem-solving action is documented and analyzed by the nursing quality assurance committee and shared with both nursing administration and staff.

# Chapter 7

# Quality Assurance and Home Health Care

## INTRODUCTION

The current emphasis on cost containment in the delivery of health care services is responsible for a steadily increasing shift from inpatient to outpatient and/or home health care. As acute care lengths of stay decrease, services that formerly required inpatient admissions are now being performed on an ambulatory or home health basis. The result of this trend is that outpatient clinics and home health agencies are seeing patients who are more acutely ill and who require a wider range of services. As hospitals diversify into non-inpatient service areas, there has been an increase in new settings that provide outpatient care.[1] Although many hospitals have organized their own programs, physicians, corporations, insurers, and other health care professionals have also developed a variety of home care services. Given the rapidly increasing need for such programs, it is important that strong quality assurance plans be implemented in these settings.

For many years, home health programs consisted primarily of nursing care.[2] Today, however, home health care is provided in multiple settings by a variety of professional disciplines working together. Rehabilitation services, which have consistently depended upon such interdisciplinary collaboration, are an integral component of today's home health environment. As the need for both rehabilitation and home health care increases, so must the emphasis on ensuring the quality of services provided.

## REHABILITATION AND HOME HEALTH CARE

About one-third of those who receive rehabilitation services have some form of neurological impairment often caused by trauma or stroke. Another third have musculoskeletal impairment such as arthritis, skeletal injuries, and amputation. The remaining third have various disabilities associated with cancer, chronic heart and lung diseases, and diabetes.[3] Many, if not most, rehabilitation patients require some community health follow up after discharge from acute care or rehabilitation facilities. Additionally, many of these patients are elderly. What impact do rehabilitation clients have on home health care organizations?

Progress in biomedical technology since World War II has better enabled health care professionals to sustain life. As more and more patients survive devastating disease and trauma with residual disabilities, and the average age of the population increases, the need for rehabilitation services will increase.[4] The need for community health services, including assistance with community reintegration, will also increase.

The fastest growing age group of the population is the elderly.[5] Those persons over 75 are more likely to need rehabilitation services. Thus, the cost of health care for the aged is consuming a large portion of the gross national product, and resources that meet those needs are being carefully monitored.[6]

Of the patients receiving home health care, 80 percent are 65 or older; 78 percent of their home care revenue is from Medicare.[7] Government and other third party payers are therefore looking for ways to obtain maximal care for minimal payment. In light of such financial pressures, and without guidelines from national standards, home health programs must be especially scrupulous in monitoring quality of care.

A significant number of physically disabled persons need personal assistance to perform activities of daily living.[8] The most important factor in helping physically disabled individuals achieve independence has been identified as personal care attendants (PCAs).[9] A PCA may be defined as a paid employee who provides in-home assistance to a severely disabled person in the areas of essential daily living activities.[10] Although most PCAs are employed directly by the disabled person and/or family, home health programs may wish to incorporate the concept in their services. This is yet another area for quality review.

Home health services must be concerned with all aspects of successful community reintegration. Disabled persons must function in the society that has been primarily designed, both architecturally and psychosocially, for nondisabled people. In order to promote optimal wellness, community health professionals must identify both facilitators and barriers to reintegration as part of the quality assurance process.

## SELF-ESTEEM, HEALTH, AND COMMUNITY REINTEGRATION

The most significant key to human behavior is the process of self-evaluation known as self-esteem. Self-esteem is essential for both health maintenance and health problem prevention.[11] The performance of daily living skills is greatly influenced by self-esteem. When an individual is confronted with circumstances where control is inhibited, a form of conditioned helplessness results.[12] The person who no longer values self may refuse to initiate the activities that are necessary to maintain health.

A number of studies have illustrated the links between self-esteem, health, and community reintegration. In the spinal cord-injured person, self-esteem may influence whether or not he or she will desire, seek, cooperate with, participate in, or successfully utilize rehabilitation services.[13] Additional support for the impact of self-esteem comes from findings that spinal cord-injured clients who score high on self-esteem scales and on the amount of satisfaction obtained from activities of daily living have fewer days of incapacitation from decubitus ulcers.[14] A 1982 study that identified the relationships of various kinds of hospitalizations to self-concept and functional independence revealed that dependent persons reflected a lower self-esteem score.[15] Factors that inhibit independence may therefore have an adverse effect upon self-esteem. What factors do disabled persons identify as inhibiting to self-esteem?

In 1980, 25 spinal cord-injured clients living in their respective communities noted that the following conditions decreased their self-worth: frustration with architectural barriers, discomfort in asking for help, alterations in body image, and dissatisfaction with education or occupation.[16] A loss of control may lead to depression, helplessness, and a decrease in self-concept. A 1980 study suggested that practice or rehearsal experiences, prior to exposure to physically or emotionally taxing real-life challenges, may exert an immunizing effect.[17]

A human being acts, feels, and performs in accordance with what is imagined to be true about oneself and one's environment. Thus, self-esteem is essential for all persons' health maintenance. The following guidelines may assist the home health professional in assessing patients' self-esteem.

- Does the patient feel able to participate in life's activities as well as most other people?
- Is the patient able to identify a number of positive qualities that he or she possesses?
- Does the patient initiate health maintenance activities (e.g., adhering to a medication regimen, skin checks for mobility-compromised persons, self-breast examinations)?
- Is the patient able to maintain eye contact during interpersonal interactions?
- Is the patient well-groomed?
- Does the patient have plans for his or her future life style (education, employment, travel, leisure activities)?
- Is the patient able to identify others with whom he or she has satisfactory interpersonal relationships? Is there an identified support system?
- Does the patient feel that he or she has control over activities of daily living (either independent performance or directing a reliable PCA)?

- Has the patient been hospitalized because of a failure to follow established health maintenance practices? If so, how many times?
- Does the patient have access to health promotion information? If so, does he or she identify health education needs? Does patient education have a positive impact on health status?
- How does the home health care industry promote the achievement and maintenance of self-esteem?

The last question may also be the most critical. An awareness of the factors that influence self-esteem may help the nurse to accelerate rehabilitation. If persons who survive the occurrence of devastating disease or trauma are not assisted to reintegrate successfully into the community, complete disengagement may result.[18]

## QUALITY, COST, AND HOME HEALTH CARE

### Evolution of Cost Concerns

Prior to the implementation of the Medicare prospective payment system in 1983, very little research was done on utilization, cost-effectiveness predictors, and the significance of home care services. The current rapid shift from inpatient to community care has brought about a swift increase in the need for home health services. Additionally, a prospective payment system for home care may be imminent. In 1985 the National Association for Home Care convened a task force to study alternative payment methods for home care.[19] Currently, the home care industry is regulated primarily by third party payers to ensure that they pay only for covered services actually rendered to the patients.[20] Alternative payment methods must be proposed in light of current expenditures.

In the 1980s, costs for home care in the United States have increased by approximately 20 to 25 percent per year.[21] Between 1980 and 1984, Medicare expenditures increased by an average rate of 29 percent per year and the cost of home health visits increased at an average rate of 9 percent per year.[22] Because of the rising demand for home health services and the simultaneously increasing cost for care, third party payers are demanding utilization review and quality monitoring to ensure that reimbursement schemes do not compromise quality of care.[23]

### Correlating Quality and Cost

Home health agencies must find ways to offer quality care while operating in a cost-efficient manner. Several agencies have published accounts of their attempts to devise systems that simultaneously promote cost containment and high quality of care.

A visiting nurse association in Pennsylvania has developed an integrated quality assurance/cost containment system based on expected patient outcomes. The system was designed to collect data about measurable changes in patient health status, knowledge, compliance, and satisfaction. Patients are classified into one of five categories, and expected outcomes are specified for each category as well as important nursing diagnoses. Upon discharge, the nurse estimates the time devoted to each nursing diagnosis, and the total cost of nursing care is divided by the time spent on each nursing diagnosis.[24] Such a system may be useful for other professional disciplines providing home health care as well.

Another system was devised as a communitywide effort to coordinate a funding structure that defined a range of home care services to be funded. Consistency was achieved in standards of care, definitions of a unit of service, the use of unit-cost reimbursements, and unit cost rates. Uniform reporting requirements were also adopted.[25]

The need for coordinating quality and cost effectiveness involves establishing measurable criteria for achieving patient outcomes within an identified funding structure. Some suggestions for organizing a system of both quality care and coordinating funding include the identification of

- patient categories (according to diagnosis, age, sex, and length of time the services were utilized)
- standardized nursing diagnoses
- measurable patient outcomes
- fee-for-service structure for all disciplines
- established standards of care
- careful utilization review
- coordination agreements with other agencies
- definitions of services provided
- means of measuring patient/family satisfaction
- patient status at time of discharge from services

## STANDARDS

Nursing quality assurance coordinators in home health should use as resources the following organizations that have developed standards applicable for nursing in the home health setting.

- Joint Commission on Accreditation of Healthcare Organizations
- National League for Nursing
- National Homecaring Council

- American Nurses' Association
- Association of Rehabilitation Nurses
- Commission on Accreditation of Rehabilitation Facilities

The National League for Nursing has developed an especially helpful document that provides home care and community health providers with criteria and standards needed to prepare self-study reports for accreditation by the League. Its purposes are

- to assist a provider to develop, interpret, improve, and evaluate all aspects of its operation
- to provide the basis for accreditation decisions
- to assure consumers that the provider has met predetermined standards relative to quality control[26]

The document covers the following areas in detail: strategic planning and marketing; organization and administration; and program, staff, and overall provider evaluation. Of particular importance to nursing quality assurance is Criterion 17: "The provider evaluates its program(s)."[27] The standard requires that there be

- an annual assessment of services, practice policies, quality of care, populations served, and patient outcomes
- a utilization review committee composed of at least one representative from each professional delivering services as well as at least one person from outside the agency
- an appraisal of a random sample of 10 percent of client records to determine appropriateness and adequacy and services.[28]

In addition to following standards as identified by professional organizations and accrediting bodies, home health nursing quality assurance personnel may want to consider developing standardized care plans. As the need for home health services grows, nursing care is "increasingly directed toward helping patients incorporate appropriate health behaviors into their life-styles."[29] The development of standardized patient care plans helps to monitor care and document patient progress in a way that meets program standards, legal guidelines, and third party payer mandates.[30]

In order to design effective standardized care plans, home health nurses must understand that in the home setting, the patient and/or family is almost always in control. Desired patient outcomes must be developed with the knowledge that the patient/family is ultimately responsible for health care. Many interventions, such as taking medications, are accomplished when health care professionals are not present. Measurable patient goals must be stated in terms of what the nurse can monitor objectively. For example, if an outcome is written that "the patient will transfer to and from the wheelchair safely," how will the nurse measure achievement? Most transfers will take place when nursing personnel are not in the home. Such a goal may be stated more effectively as "the patient will demonstrate safe transfer techniques to and from the wheelchair." A return demonstration is only one way of assessing achievement. The incidence of falls, injuries, and patient/family reports of problems during transfers are other methods of monitoring.

If a home health agency decides to initiate standardized patient care plans, some points to remember are:

- Care plans should be based on programmatic standards that direct nursing practice in the home health setting.
- Care plans should facilitate documentation that adheres to legal guidelines, professional standards, accrediting body standards, and third party payer requirements.
- Care plans should facilitate the documentation of patient education and its impact on patient/family behaviors.
- Patient/family outcomes must be written in terms of behaviors that the nurse can measure objectively.
- Each outcome should have a time frame for achievement.
- Care plans should be reviewed and revised at least annually

Exhibits 7-1 and 7-2 illustrate a portion of a sample standardized care plan and its accompanying patient/family education record. There are identified outcomes for each intervention in the care plan. The education record identifies methods of instruction for each outcome. Each teaching session is numbered and dated. The instructor evaluating the session writes the appropriate code and initials in the space provided. Such standardized care plans and teaching records provide a consistent, simplified means of monitoring care and ensuring acceptable documentation.

## ASSESSMENT AND PLANNING

### Introduction

Like rehabilitation, successful home health programs need centralization of interdisciplinary workings. A fragmented program, with each discipline functioning independently in terms of monitoring and evaluation, will fail to promote

**Exhibit 7-1**  Standardized Care Plan

DIABETES MANAGEMENT

| Nursing Diagnosis | Outcome | Interventions |
|---|---|---|
| Knowledge deficit regarding | Patient will complete pre-test within 5 days | Administer pre-test |
| (1) Disease process | Patient will define diabetes and describe its signs and symptoms within 1 week | Provide definition of diabetes, its signs, and symptoms |
| (2) Medication regimen | Patient will describe hyper- and hypoglycemic reactions within 10 days | Explain signs, symptoms, and causes of hyper- and hypoglycemic reactions |
| | Patient will describe action and side effects of hypoglycemic agent within 12 days | Teach action and side effects of medication |
| | Patient will demonstrate accurate self-injection of insulin within 3 weeks | Instruct patient in accurate insulin-injection technique |
| | Patient will pass post-test within 4 weeks with a minimum score of 90% | Administer post-test |

**Exhibit 7-2** Patient/Family Education Record

DIABETES MANAGEMENT

| Outcome | Content | Method | Session # Date/ | Session # Date/ | Session # Date/ |
|---------|---------|--------|-----------------|-----------------|-----------------|
| Patient will complete pre-test within 5 days | Administer pre-test | 1:1 instruction | | | |
| Patient will define diabetes and describe its signs and symptoms within 1 week | Provide definition of diabetes, its signs, and symptoms | Handouts Explanations | | | |
| Patient will describe hyper- and hypoglycemic reactions within 10 days | Explain signs, symptoms, and causes of hyper- and hypoglycemic reactions | Handouts Explanations | | | |
| Patient will describe action and side effects of hypoglycemic agent within 12 days | Teach action and side effects of medications | Handouts Video Explanations | | | |

Initials _____ Signatures _____
_____
_____
_____

Evaluation Code
S = Satisfactory
U = Unsatisfactory
N/A = Non-applicable

uniformity of high-quality care. Each discipline, although maintaining its own standards of professional practice, must contribute to the overall evaluation of home health services. Nursing, when developing standardized care plans, for instance, must consider how these plans will interface with the *total* plan of interdisciplinary home health services. Planning quality assurance activities in this setting should begin with a review of the following key issues and how they may influence quality care.

- Home health services are provided in a variety of settings over which caregivers often have little or no control. Patients' homes provide one of the greatest challenges to the provision of services. Environmental issues may severely hamper the provision of quality care.
  1. Does the home setting have adequate hygiene facilities?
  2. Is the patient confined to a specific area of the home? Are bathroom facilities accessible in that area?
  3. If the patient needs assistance to perform activities of daily living, is there someone in the home setting to provide help? Is this family caregiver able and willing to provide the necessary assistance? Are there alternative means of help if the primary caregiver is temporarily unable to help the patient? Do the patient and caregiver(s) know how to summon necessary help in an emergency (sudden severe illness, fire, theft, etc.)?
  4. Is the home setting conducive to health care provision? Are there steps to get into and/or move throughout the home? Is the setting accessible to the patient, family, and home health care provider? What safety hazards exist in the home? Can they be rendered less harmful?
  5. How does the home health care team attempt to help make the environment more conducive to health maintenance? How is this documented? How is success measured?
  6. Does the home health organization operate any outpatient services from a clinic? If so, how is outpatient care of this type evaluated?
- Home health services are provided by a variety of professional disciplines.
  1. How is the provision of services coordinated? Is a variety of services provided on the same day that may tire the patient?
  2. Are there regular interdisciplinary team meetings to ensure consistency of approach to treatment? Are all disciplines utilizing a similar foundation for therapeutic treatment (e.g., Bobath approach for care of the stroke patient)? Are there team goals in conjunction with discipline goals?
  3. Is each discipline represented on the quality assurance committee? How

are the results of quality assurance activities communicated to the staff? Are all levels (both professional and nonprofessional) involved in the quality assurance process?

- Financial constraints influence not only services provided but the ability of patient and families to carry out health maintenance practices.
    1. Are home health services financed by a third party payer? If not, are the costs of services a burden to the patient and family?
    2. Are special equipment and supplies necessary for health maintenance? Can the patient afford them? Is the patient willing to spend money for supplies identified as necessary by home health care providers?
- In the home health setting, services are not easily observed by a supervisor.
    1. How do supervisors evaluate their subordinates' performance? Is this done at regularly established intervals? Do supervisors visit the home settings as part of the evaluation process?
    2. Are patients and families given opportunities to evaluate services? Is this done both during and after completion of services? Are both verbal and written input taken into consideration?
    3. Is documentation part of the evaluation process? Are documentation standards explicit?
    4. Are performance evaluations based on clearly identified outcome criteria?

These issues illustrate the unique factors impacting on the provision of quality care in the home health setting. In the inpatient setting, environmental control is usually maintained by the health care team, and services are easily observed by supervisory personnel. In the home health setting, the opposite is the case. These factors must be considered throughout all phases of any home health quality assurance program.

## Patient Needs

Home health provides services to persons of all ages. Quality assurance must measure adequacy of care in conjunction with the special needs of each age group. The numbers of persons who live with various types of physical disabilities are increasing. As the average life span increases, so does the incidence of chronic illnesses that require home health intervention. Hospice care needs are also increasing, as patients and families help each other through the final stages of terminal illnesses. Home health care providers should monitor the appropriateness of their programs in light of developmental needs throughout the life span.

Quality assurance monitors may also be categorized according to specific groupings of patient problems. What are the most frequently identified problems requiring home health intervention? Examples of factors to be monitored on an ongoing basis may include

- safety problems, including falls, burns, misuse of equipment, or signs and symptoms of complications
- medication errors, including administration by staff, patient, and/or caregivers
- skin breakdown
- patient and/or caregiver refusing services
- noncompliance of patient and/or caregiver with treatment regimen
- return of patient to an acute inpatient setting
- adverse reactions to medication or other treatment measures
- identified knowledge deficits and measures to correct them
- patient/family dissatisfaction

These problems may be more specifically detailed according to standardized care plans. Safety hazards and treatment measures may be related to specific diagnostic categories for ease of monitoring and documentation.

## Administrative Needs

The administrative aspects of managing a home health agency are also part of a sound quality assurance program. Management issues for ongoing monitoring include

- screening for appropriateness of referral
- staff recruitment and retention
- staff performance
- continuing education for staff
- documentation
- compliance with reimbursement regulations
- compliance with program standards
- adequacy of equipment and supplies

Monitoring activities should involve not only the home health program as a whole, but performances of individual disciplines as well. Such a thorough monitoring process requires careful implementation, beginning with the quality assurance committee structure itself.

## IMPLEMENTATION

### Committee Structure

The quality assurance committee format may be organized in a discipline-specific manner, as a centralized committee with a representative from each discipline, or, most effectively, as a combination of both. Nursing quality assurance activities may be coordinated as a department-specific committee with representation from each level of nursing personnel (e.g., registered nurse, licensed practical nurse, health assistant). The chairperson will most likely be the director or assistant director of nursing services. The chairperson maintains responsibility for directing the nursing quality assurance program and ensuring that it interfaces smoothly with the agency's total quality assurance endeavors.

The agency quality assurance program should consist of representatives from each discipline. These representatives should be the chairpersons of the discipline-specific quality assurance committees.

The responsibility of chairing the meetings for the agency program may be rotated—on a yearly basis, for example—among the members or may be assumed by the agency administrator. The key element for the success of quality assurance activities is their impact on improving the quality and appropriateness of care. Regardless of committee format, quality assurance activities must be coordinated so that all services are monitored adequately. In summary, such activities must show that the home health agency personnel

- demonstrate viability as an organization
- coordinate the services of a variety of disciplines so that the program of care is consistent and is reinforced by all agency workers in the individual home setting
- monitor and evaluate risks to both patient/family and employees
- maintain fiscal and cost containment responsibility
- promote patient/family rights as partners in designing treatment plans
- adhere to agency, federal, state, accrediting body, and professional organization standards
- develop effective means of communication with referral sources
- participate in the review and revision of agency programs

## Goals

Quality assurance goals must be both realistic and measurable as well as objectively evaluative. Each of these characteristics takes on special aspects when part of a home health program.

- Realistic. As previously mentioned, the staff has little or no control in the home setting. Goals that require extensive and costly environmental adaptations are not achievable if the patient's financial status does not allow for them. Goals that require interventions that are beyond the patient's/caregiver's understanding are useless. Each family's situation must be considered individually. Goals must be formulated from the patient's/family's perspective, not exclusively from what staff members deem desirable.
- Measurable. Goals may be measured by return demonstrations, explanations, post-tests, or resulting changes in health status. A quality assurance goal stating that 90 percent of patients will comply with their medication regimens cannot be measured as stated since most compliance takes place when staff members are not present in the home. A better way of formulating the goal might be that 90 percent of patients/caregivers will be able to identify medication(s) by sight, identify the time frame for administration, and describe the signs and symptoms of adverse side effects.
- Objectively evaluative. The key to appropriate evaluation is objectivity. After goals are stated in measurable terms, the evaluation process is directly correlated with them. Using the previous example under the characteristics of measurable goals, agency personnel might listen to the patient/caregiver identify and describe medication(s), time frames, and adverse effects. Further means of evaluating actual compliance would include monitoring desired effects of medication. For example, if medication includes an antihypertensive, blood pressure readings within normal limits and reports of adverse occurrences (as a result of either too much or too little medication) are objective means of evaluating compliance. All quality assurance goals must incorporate methods of monitoring success in situations where the agency staff members are absent more than they are present.

## Monitoring and Evaluating Program Quality

Program monitors may be organized in three categories: administrative, discipline-specific, and interdiscipline-oriented. The following examples illustrate the monitoring and evaluation process in each case.

*Administrative*

Documentation is the primary communication vehicle between health care providers and is the means of recording adherence to program standards. Table 7-1 illustrates a partial monitoring plan for some documentation issues of particular importance to administrative personnel. These considerations may include

- team review of referral appropriateness within an identified time frame of service initiation
- identification of the patient's primary physician upon initiation of services
- maintenance of copies of all transfer and summary reports at the time home health services are initiated
- review and revision of the patient care plan by the home health care team, including the patient's primary physician, at regularly scheduled intervals
- assessment of adaptability of the patients' homes for provided services within 48 hours of the initial visit
- documentation of discipline and/or team treatment plan within 48 hours of the initial visit

Results from Table 7-1 show that the criterion for documentation of treatment plans was not achieved. The actions taken might include

- Identification of discipline(s) responsible. Examine the records of patients whose treatment plans were not documented within the required 48 hours. Are there identifiable trends? Are particular disciplines routinely late in their documentation? Are certain staff members routinely delinquent in documenting treatment plans? If the problem can be narrowed to an identifiable department, these staff members must be immediately involved in the problem-solving process. Are these staff members carrying an especially heavy patient load? Are there staffing shortages affecting services?
- Review of patient characteristics. Are there notable trends in patient characteristics? Were there difficulties in formulating treatment plans due to referral appropriateness or lack of patient/family input? Were there problems gaining entry to patients' homes? If so, what were the difficulties?
- Discussion with staff. How did the staff members perceive documentation problems? Did they identify problems with the documentation format? Did they note particular problems with patients or with staffing patterns? Do they see the documentation deficiencies as a short-term problem or a continuing problem? What suggestions do they have for correcting the problem?

**Table 7-1** Sample Administrative Monitoring Plan: Monthly Report, January 1989

| Monitor | Criterion | Result | Analysis | Action |
|---|---|---|---|---|
| Percentage of referral appropriateness reviews within 7 working days of service initiation | 100% | 100% | Criterion achieved | Continue to monitor |
| Upon initiation of services, the percentage of patients whose primary physician is clearly identified | 100% | 100% | Criterion achieved | Continue to monitor |
| Percentage of treatment plans documented within 48 hours of initial visit | 100% | 88% | Criterion not achieved | 1. Identify discipline(s) responsible<br>2. Review patient characteristics<br>3. Discuss with staff<br>4. Make recommendations |

- Action plan
  1. Identify trends involving particular disciplines and/or staff members.
  2. Review staff availability and any staff shortages, and determine whether certain staff members are unfamiliar with documentation guidelines.
  3. Review patient characteristics for referral appropriateness, cooperation of patient/family, or difficulties in formulating treatment plan.
  4. Review documentation format for appropriateness.
  5. Involve the staff in problem-correcting activities. Incorporate staff recommendations in all of the above steps.

## Discipline-Specific

Table 7-2 shows a nursing monitoring plan for some of the diabetes management interventions. Based on information in Exhibits 7-1 and 7-2, a monitoring system can be developed to correlate with a standardized care plan. Specific nursing interventions center on the problem of knowledge deficit. They involve

- assisting the patient in the completion of a pretest to assess initial knowledge base
- providing the patient with a definition of diabetes as well as its signs and symptoms
- assisting the patient to describe hyper- and hypoglycemic reactions
- helping the patient to describe the action and side effects of hypoglycemic agents
- assisting the patient (as appropriate) to self-administer insulin accurately
- administering a post-test to help measure the success of the teaching program

Analysis shows that the criterion established for a written post-test score was not achieved. Action might include a nursing review of

- Patient characteristics. The nursing personnel involved in this patient education program should assess the patient's/family's readiness and willingness to learn. Are there family dynamics interfering with the learning process? Was the information presented in a way that the patient/family could understand? Was the patient's baseline knowledge carefully assessed? Did the patient/family have an opportunity to evaluate the teaching program? What was the patient's educational background?
- Teaching plan. How was the teaching plan implemented? Was there more than one nurse involved in the teaching process? Were they consistent in

**Table 7-2** Monitoring Plan for Diabetes Management: First Quarter Report, 1989

| Monitor | Criterion | Result | Analysis | Action |
|---|---|---|---|---|
| Percentage of patients/ families able to define diabetes, its signs, and symptoms within 1 week | 95% | 98% | Criterion achieved | Continue to monitor |
| Percentage of patients/ families able to describe the action and side effects of the hypoglycemic agent | 95% | 95% | Crietrion achieved | Continue to monitor |
| Percentage of patients/ families able to administer insulin accurately (as appropriate) | 95% | 95% | Criterion achieved | Continue to monitor |
| Percentage of patients/ families completing post-test: written portion 90% practicum, pass | Practicum 100% Written 90% | 100% 85% | Criterion achieved Criterion not achieved | Continue to monitor Review: 1. Patient characteristics 2. Teaching plan 3. Quality of written test Formulate plan |

their adherence to the teaching plan? Were there any changes in the program based on patient needs? How were these needs assessed? Was the plan individualized to meet patient/family needs? If not, why not?

- Quality of the written test. Is the test written in a manner that is comprehensible to the average patient/family? Is the terminology interfering with patient/family understanding? How have the nurses involved compensated for a patient/family's difficulty in reading and understanding the written test? Was there consistency of approach?

- Action plan
    1. Review the suitability of the written test. Seek assistance from educational experts as necessary.
    2. Review patient/family evaluations of the teaching program in general and of the written test in particular.
    3. Have the staff review feedback and revise the program and test as needed.
    4. Have the staff review their teaching efforts, and revise interventions as needed.
    5. Have the staff review patient/family characteristics, and review possible alternatives to the written test based on specific criteria.
    6. Review test results again within one month.

## Interdiscipline-Oriented

Table 7-3 illustrates a portion of a sample interdisciplinary monitoring plan for home health follow up of patients with spinal cord injury. Consistency of the team (nursing, physical therapy, and occupational therapy) approach is necessary for successful outcomes. All staff members must contribute to the plan as measured by the following monitors.

- Patient/family report of falls. Since team members are not present as all activities are conducted, a report of falls and evidence of injury are the most objective means of noting the incidence of falls.

- Patient/family report of symptoms of urinary tract infections. A urinary tract infection may indicate noncompliance in patient/family performance of intermittent catheterizations.

- Incidence of skin breakdown. Skin breakdown may indicate insufficient teaching or inability of patients/caregivers to carry out skin maintenance programs.

Analysis of the plan shows that there was an unacceptable incidence of skin breakdown. Team measures to correct the plan might include a review of

**Table 7-3** Interdiscipline-Oriented Plan for Spinal Cord Injury: First Quarter, 1989

| Monitor | Criterion | Result | Analysis | Action |
|---|---|---|---|---|
| Percentage of patients/families reporting incidence of falls | Less than 5% | 4.5% | Criterion achieved | Continue to monitor |
| Percentage of patients/families reporting signs and symptoms of urinary tract infection | Less than 10% | 9% | Criterion achieved | Continue to monitor |
| Percentage of patients/families reporting incidence of skin breakdown | 0% | 5% | Criterion not achieved | Review:<br>1. Patient/family characteristics<br>2. Team intervention<br>3. Plan of action |

- Patient/family characteristics. Are there similarities among patients/families who experience skin breakdowns? If so, what are they? Was information concerning skin breakdown presented in an understandable manner, individualized to meet patient/family needs? Were patients/families involved in the plan of care and in evaluating its effectiveness?
- Team interventions. Were certain team members involved with patients who experienced skin breakdown? Was there a break in consistency of teaching? Was patient/family feedback solicited throughout the teaching/learning process?
- Action plan
  1. Review teaching interventions regarding skin breakdown.
  2. Assess interventions; especially monitor to determine whether they are individualized to meet patient/family needs.
  3. Solicit patient/family input regarding problems with intact skin maintenance.
  4. Revise interventions as necessary.
  5. Assess the monitor again within one month.
  6. Ensure that all team members continue to be involved in the monitoring/evaluation process.

In summary, a successful monitoring and evaluation process is based on successful team interaction with patients/families and a willingness to adapt the plan of care to meet individualized patient needs.

## INDICATIONS FOR RESEARCH

Research may be used to enhance the effectiveness of services, staff satisfaction, and cost containment. Some indications for research include

- factors that influence costs of services, both team-oriented and discipline-specific
- how interventions impact on patient/family outcomes
- how patients' caregivers influence the success of patient outcomes
- how referral sources influence the success of treatment measures
- factors that impact on staff recruitment and retention

## SUMMARY

The emphasis on the delivery of health care services is shifting from inpatient to outpatient and home health sites. As the need for such services increases, the need for adequate quality assurance programs also increases.

Factors that especially influence the delivery of quality home health care include a wide variety of delivery settings, patient/family compliance that is usually not directly observable by the staff, the coordination of care by diverse disciplines, and the inability to directly supervise the staff. By establishing monitoring plans concerning administrative, discipline-specific, and team-oriented interventions, a quality assurance program should be able to assess accurately the quality and appropriateness of services provided.

NOTES

1. Clare E. Hastins, "Measuring Quality in Ambulatory Care Nursing," *Journal of Nursing Administration* 17, no. 4 (1987): 12.

2. Julie L. Hopkins, ed., "Increased Quality and Reduced Risk in the Home Care Setting," in *QRC Advisor* 3, no. 10 (August 1987): 1.

3. Arthur L. Caplan, Daniel Callahan, and Janet Haas, *Ethical and Policy Issues in Rehabilitation Medicine*. A Hastings Center Report—special supplement derived from the Hastings Center Project on Ethical Issues in Rehabilitation Medicine (Briarcliff Manor, N.Y.: Hastings Center, 1987), 1.

4. Kathleen Mitchell, "The Rehabilitation Client: Considerations for Home Care," *Rehabilitation Nursing* 12 (1987): 255.

5. Ibid.

6. J. Avorn, "Benefit and Cost Analysis in Geriatric Care: Turning Age Discrimination into Health Policy," *New England Journal of Medicine* 310 (1984): 1294–1301.

7. Hopkins, "Increased Quality and Reduced Risk in the Home Care Setting," 1.

8. Elaine L. Miller and Nancy D. Opie, "Severely Disabled Adults and Personal Care Attendants: A Pilot Study," *Rehabilitation Nursing* 12 (1987): 185.

9. N.K. Smith and A.B. Meyer, "Personal Care Attendants: Key to Living Independently," *Rehabilitation Literature* 42 (1981): 258–265.

10. R.K. Hutchins et al., "Profile of In-Home Attendant Care Workers," *American Rehabilitation* (1978): 18–22.

11. Adrianne E. Avillion, "Barrier Perception and Its Influence on Self-Esteem," *Rehabilitation Nursing* 11 (1986): 11.

12. R.N. Wool and D. Siegel, "Task Performance in Spinal Cord Injury: Effects of Helplessness Training," *Archives of Physical Medicine and Rehabilitation* 61 (1980): 321–324.

13. A.D. Mueller, "Psychologic Factors in Rehabilitation of Paraplegic Patients," *Archives of Physical Medicine and Rehabilitation* 43 (1962): 151–159.

14. R.B. Trieschman, *The Psychological, Social, and Vocational Adjustment in Spinal Cord Injury: A Strategy for Future Research*. Final report, grant number 13-P-59011-9-01 Rehabilitation Services Administration, Department of Health, Education, and Welfare, Washington, and Easter Seal Society of Los Angeles County, Los Angeles, 1978.

15. M.J. Aitken, "Self-Concept and Functional Independence in the Hospitalized Elderly," *Ameri-*

*can Journal of Occupational Therapy* 36 (1982): 243–250.

16. R.L. Starch, "Maslow's Needs and the Spinal Cord Injured Client," *Rehabilitation Nursing* 5, no. 5 (1980): 17–20.

17. Wool and Siegel, "Task Performance in Spinal Cord Injury," 321–324.

18. B. Goldiamond, "Resocialization," in *Comprehensive Rehabilitation Nursing*, ed. N. Martin, N. Holt, and O. Hicks (New York: McGraw-Hill Book Co., 1981), 697–728.

19. Debra K. Pasquale, "A Basis for Prospective Payment for Home Care," *Image: Journal of Nursing Scholarship* 19, no. 4 (Winter 1987): 186.

20. Helen Heyrman, "Home Care Quality Assurance: Dollars and Sense or Dollars and Cents?" *Home Healthcare Nurse* 5, no. 2 (1987): 8.

21. Nancy L. Mumma, "Quality and Cost Control of Home Care Services through Coordinated Funding," *Quality Review Bulletin* 13 (1987): 271.

22. W. Kirby, V. Latta, and C. Helbing, "Medicare Use and Cost of Home Health Agency Services," *Health Care Financing Review* 8 (1983–1984): 93–100.

23. Marilyn D. Harris, Donna A. Peters, and Joan Yuan, "Relating Quality and Cost in a Home Health Care Agency," *Quality Review Bulletin* 13 (1987): 175–181.

24. Ibid.

25. Mumma, "Quality and Cost Control of Home Care Services," 273–274.

26. Accreditation Division for Home Care and Community Health, National League for Nursing, *Accreditation Criteria Standards and Substantiating Evidences* (New York: National League for Nursing, 1987), 1.

27. Ibid., 29.

28. Ibid.

29. E. Joyce Gould, "Standardized Home Health Nursing Care Plans: A Quality Assurance Tool," *Quality Review Bulletin* (November 1985): 334.

30. Ibid.

---

## BIBLIOGRAPHY

Bernal, Henrietta, and Froman, Robin. "The Confidence of Community Health Nurses in Caring for Ethnically Diverse Populations." *Image: Journal of Nursing Scholarship* 19, no. 4 (1987): 201–203.

Christopher, Mary Ann. "Home Care for the Elderly." *Nursing 86* 16, no. 7 (July 1986): 50–55.

Daniels, Kaye. "Planning for Quality in the Home Care System." *Quality Review Bulletin* 12, no. 7 (1986): 247–251.

Droste, Therese. "Medicare Denials Threaten the Health of Home Care." *Hospitals* 5 (June 1987): 58.

Gould, E. Joyce. "Standardized Home Health Nursing Care Plans: A Quality Assurance Tool." *Quality Review Bulletin* 11, no. 11 (1985): 334–338.

Harris, Marilyn D.; Peters, Donna A.; and Yuan, Joan. "Relating Quality and Cost in a Home Health Care Agency." *Quality Review Bulletin* 13, no. 5 (1987): 175–181.

Heyrman, Helen. "Home Care Quality Assurance: Dollars and Sense or Dollars and Cents?" *Home Healthcare Nurse* 5, no. 2 (1987): 8–9.

Hopkins, Julie L., ed. "Increased Quality and Reduced Risk in the Home Care Setting." *QRC Advisor* 3, no. 10 (1987): 1–2, 5–7.

Ingram, Helen H., and Harmon, Robert G. "Quality Assurance in a Public Health Agency." *Quality Review Bulletin* 13, no. 11 (1987): 372–376.

Joint Commission on Accreditation of Healthcare Organizations. *Monitoring and Evaluation of the Quality and Appropriateness of Care.* Chicago: Joint Commission on Accreditation of Healthcare Organizations, 1986.

Lalonde, Bernadette. "The General Symptom Distress Scale: A Home Care Outcome Measure." *Quality Review Bulletin* 13, no. 7 (1987): 243–250.

Long, Hugh W. "Home Health Care: Payment and Growth." *Physician Executive* 14, no. 3 (1988): 27–28.

Miller, Elaine L., and Opie, Nancy D. "Severely Disabled Adults and Personal Care Attendants: A Pilot Study." *Rehabilitation Nursing* 12, no. 4 (1987): 185–187.

Mumma, Nancy L. "Quality and Cost Control of Home Care Services through Coordinated Funding." *Quality Review Bulletin* 13, no. 8 (1987): 271–278.

Oswald, Eileen, and Inge, K. Winer. "A Simple Approach to Quality Assurance in a Complex Ambulatory Care Setting." *Quality Review Bulletin* 13, no. 2 (1987): 56–60.

Pasquale, Debra K. "A Basis for Prospective Payment for Home Care." *Image: Journal of Nursing Scholarship* 19, no. 4 (1987): 186–191.

Rinke, Lynn T., ed. *Outcome Measures in Home Care. Vol. I: Research.* New York: National League for Nursing, 1987.

Rinke, Lynn T., and Wilson, Alexis A., eds. *Outcome Measures in Home Care. Vol. II: Service.* New York: National League for Nursing, 1987.

Siu, Albert L. "The Quality of Medical Care Received by Older Persons." *Journal of American Geriatric Society* 35, no. 12 (1987): 1084–1091.

Smith Marker, Carolyn G. "The Marker Model: A Hierarchy for Nursing Standards." *Journal of Nursing Quality Assurance* 1, no. 2 (1987): 7–20.

## SUGGESTED READINGS

Affeldt, John E., and Walczak, Regina M. "The Role of JCAH in Assuring Quality Care." In *Hospital Quality Assurance Risk Management and Program Evaluation*, edited by Jesus J. Pena, Alden N. Haffner, Bernard Rosen, and Donald W. Light. Rockville, Md.: Aspen Publishers, Inc., 1984.

Alder, M., and Brown, C.C. Jr. "Who Reviews the Reviewers? A Retrospective Study of Medicare Determinations." *New England Journal of Medicine* 302, no. 15 (1980): 842–844.

American Nurses' Association. *Standards of Community Health Nursing Practice.* Kansas City, Mo.: American Nurses' Association, 1986.

Asberg, K.H. "Assessment of ADL in Home-Care for the Elderly." *Scandinavian Journal of Social Medicine* 14 (1986): 105–111.

Avorn, J. "Benefit and Cost Analysis in Geriatric Care; Turning Age Discrimination into Health Policy." *New England Journal of Medicine* 310, no. 20 (1984): 1294–1301.

Ballard, S., and McNamara, R. "Quantifying Nursing Needs in Home Health Care." *Nursing Research* 32 (1983): 236–241.

Bloch, Doris. "Evaluation of Nursing Care in Terms of Process and Outcome: Issues in Research and Quality Assurance." *Nursing Research* 24 (July/August 1975): 256–263.

Bloch, Doris. "Interrelated Issues in Evaluation and Evaluation Research: A Researcher's Perspective." *Nursing Research* 29 (1980): 69–73.

Bohnet, Nancy L. "Quality Assurance As an Ongoing Component of Hospice Care." *Quality Review*

*Bulletin* 8, no. 5 (1982): 7–11.

Brody, E.M. "Parent Care as a Normative Family Stress." *Gerontologist* 25 (1985): 19–29.

Brook, R.H., and Lohr, K.N. "Quality of Care Assessment: Its Role in the 1980's." *American Journal of Public Health* 71 (1981): 681–682.

Brook, R.H., and Williams, K.N. "Quality of Health Care for the Disadvantaged." *Journal of Community Health* 1 (1975): 132–156.

Bruskewitz, Mary A. "Observation As an Evaluation Tool." In *Nursing Quality Assurance: A Unit-Based Approach*, edited by Patricia S. Schroeder and Regina M. Maibusch. Rockville, Md.: Aspen Publishers, Inc., 1984.

Churness, V.H.; Keffel, D.; Jacobson, J.; and Onodera, M. "Development of a Patient Classification System for Home Health Nursing." In *Patient and Purse Strings*, edited by F.A. Shaffer. New York: National League for Nursing, 1986.

Culp, Barbara; Goemaere, Nathalie D.; and Miller, M. Eldoris. "Risk Management: An Integral Part of Quality Assurance." In *Quality Assurance: A Complete Guide to Effective Programs*, edited by Claire G. Meisenheimer. Rockville, Md.: Aspen Publishers, Inc., 1985.

Daniels, Kaye. "Planning for Quality in the Home Care System." *Quality Review Bulletin* 12 (July 1986): 247–251.

Davis-Martin, S. "Outcome and Accountability: Getting into the Consumer Dimension." *Nursing Management* 17, no. 10 (1986): 25–29.

Donabedian, Avedis. "Some Basic Issues in Evaluating the Quality of Health Care." In *Issues in Evaluation Research*. Kansas City, Mo.: American Nurses' Association, 1976, 3.

Driever, Marie J. "Interpretation: A Critical Component of the Quality Assurance Process." *Journal of Nursing Quality Assurance* 2, no. 2 (1988): 55–58.

Falvo, Donna R. "Patient Education As a Process in Patient Care." In *Effective Patient Education: A Guide to Increased Compliance*. Rockville, Md.: Aspen Publishers, Inc., 1985.

Falvo, Donna R. "Psychosocial Factors and Patient Compliance." In *Effective Patient Education: A Guide to Increased Compliance*. Rockville, Md.: Aspen Publishers, Inc., 1985.

Falvo, Donna R. "The Family in Patient Education." In *Effective Patient Education: A Guide to Increased Compliance*. Rockville, Md.: Aspen Publishers, Inc., 1985.

Fortinsky, R.H.; Granger, C.V.; and Seltzer, G.B. "The Use of Functional Assessment in Understanding Home Care Needs." *Medical Care* 19 (1981): 489–499.

Frederick, Bruce J.; Sharp, Judeann Q.; and Atkins, Natalie. "Quality of Patient Care: Whose Decision?" *Journal of Nursing Quality Assurance* 2, no. 3 (May 1988): 1–9.

Friedman, J.A. "Guiding Patients through the Labyrinth of Home Health Care Services." *Nursing Health Care* 7, no. 6 (1986): 304–306.

Fries, B.F., and Cooney, L.M. "Resource Utilization Groups: A Patient Classification System for Long-Term Care." *Medical Care* 23 (1985): 110–122.

Griffith, D.G. "Blending Key Ingredients To Assure Quality in Home Health Care." *Nursing Health Care* 7, no. 6 (1986): 300–302.

Griffith, N.A., and Megel, M.E. "Quality Assurance: An Educational Approach." *Nursing Outlook* 29 (1981): 670–673.

Hankes, D.D. "Self Care: Assessing the Aged Client's Need for Independence." *Journal of Gerontologic Nursing* 10 (1984): 27–31.

Hastings, Clare E. "Measuring Quality in Ambulatory Care Nursing." *Journal of Nursing Administration* 17, no. 4 (1987): 12–20.

Hexum, J. "Monitoring Standards Instead of Problems." *Journal of Nursing Quality Assurance* 1, no.

3 (1987); 8–13.

Heyrman, Helen. "Home Care Quality Assurance: Dollars and Sense or Dollars and Cents?" *Home Healthcare Nurse* 5, no. 2 (1987): 8–9.

Hill, Barbara A.; Johnson, Ruth; and Garrett, Betty J. "Reducing the Incidence of Falls in High Risk Patients." *Journal of Nursing Administration* 13, no. 7/8 (July/August 1988): 24–28.

Holsinger, James W. "Cost versus Quality." In *Hospital Quality Assurance Risk Management and Program Evaluation*, edited by Jesus J. Pena, Alden N. Haffner, Bernard Rosen, and Donald W. Light. Rockville, Md.: Aspen Publishers, Inc., 1984.

Hopkins, Julie L., ed. "Increased Quality and Reduced Risk in the Home Care Setting." *QRC Advisor* 3, no. 10 (August 1987): 1–2, 5–7.

Hughes, S.L. "Home Health Monitoring: Ensuring Quality in Home Care Services." *Hospitals* 56, no. 21 (1982): 74–80.

Hutchins, R.K.; Thornock, M.; Lindgren, B.; and Parks, J. "Profile of In-Home Attendant Care Workers." *American Rehabilitation* 4, no. 2 (November/December 1978): 18–22.

Ingram, Helen H., and Harmon, Robert G. "Quality Assurance in a Public Health Agency." *Quality Review Bulletin* 13, no. 11 (November 1987): 372–376.

Johnson, E. "Accidental Falls among Geriatric Patients: Can More Be Prevented?" *Journal of National Medical Association* 77, no. 8 (1985): 633–639.

Joint Commission on Accreditation of Healthcare Organizations. *Accreditation Manual for Hospitals/88*. Chicago: Joint Commission on Accreditation of Healthcare Organizations, 1987.

Kanar, Richard J. "The Influence of a Quality Assurance Program on Patient Satisfaction." *Journal of Nursing Quality Assurance* 2, no. 3 (1988): 36–43.

Kirby, W.; Latta, V.; and Helbing, C. "Medicare Use and Cost of Home Health Agency Services, 1983–1984." *Health Care Financing Report* 8 (Fall 1986): 93–100.

Krueger, Janelle C. "Establishing Priorities for Evaluation and Evaluation Research: A Nursing Perspective." *Nursing Research* 9, no. 29 (1980): 115–118.

Larson, E. "Combining Nursing Quality Assurance and Research Programs." *Journal of Nursing Administration* 13 (1983): 33.

Lewis, Ellen M. "Administration Support." In *Quality Assurance: A Complete Guide to Effective Programs*, edited by Claire G. Meisenheimer. Rockville, Md.: Aspen Publishers, Inc., 1985.

Lieske, Anna Marie. "Quality Assurance and Research." In *Quality Assurance: A Complete Guide to Effective Programs*, edited by Claire Gavin Meisenheimer. Rockville, Md.: Aspen Publishers, Inc., 1985.

Lieske, Anna Marie. "Reporting Mechanisms." In *Quality Assurance: A Complete Guide to Effective Programs*, edited by Claire Gavin Meisenheimer. Rockville, Md.: Aspen Publishers, Inc., 1985.

Lieske, Anna Marie. "Standards: The Basis of a Quality Assurance Program." In *Quality Assurance: A Complete Guide to Effective Programs*, edited by Claire Gavin Meisenheimer. Rockville, Md.: Aspen Publishers, Inc., 1985.

Linn, M.W.; Gurel L.; and Linn, B.S. "Patient Outcome As a Measure of Quality of Nursing Home Care." *American Journal of Public Health* 67 (April 1977): 337–344.

Long, Hugh W. "Home Health Care: Payment and Growth." *Physician Executive* 14, no. 3 (1988): 27–28.

Maciorowski, Linda F. "Quality Assurance Data: Whose Information Is It Anyway?" *Journal of Nursing Quality Assurance* 2, no. 3 (1988): 18–21.

Maciorowski, Linda F.; Larson, Elaine; and Kearne, Anne. "Quality Assurance Evaluate Thyself." *Journal of Nursing Administration* 15, no. 6 (June 1985): 38–42.

Marriner, Ann. *The Nursing Process: A Scientific Approach to Nursing Care*. 3rd ed. St. Louis: C.V. Mosby Co., 1983.

McCann, B.A., and Hill, K.A. "The JCAH Home Care Project." *Quality Review Bulletin* 12, no. 5 (1986): 191–193.

Megel, Mary Erickson, and Elrod, Mary E. Barna. "Quality Assurance: Taking a New Look at Collaboration between Education and Service." *Journal of Nursing Quality Assurance* 2, no. 1 (1987): 65–73.

Meisenheimer, Claire Gavin, ed. "Designing a Quality Assurance Program." In *Quality Assurance: A Complete Guide to Effective Programs*. Rockville, Md.: Aspen Publishers, Inc., 1985.

Miller, Elaine L., and Opie, Nancy D. "Severely Disabled Adults and Personal Care Attendants: A Pilot Study." *Rehabilitation Nursing* 12, no. 4 (1987): 185–187.

Mitchell, Kathleen. "The Rehabilitation Client: Considerations for Home Care." *Rehabilitation Nursing* 12, no. 5 (1987): 255–256.

Mosbeth, Robin Reading. "A Practical Guide to Multidisciplinary Auditing." In *Nursing Quality Assurance: A Unit-Based Approach*, edited by Patricia S. Schroeder and Regina M. Maibusch. Rockville, Md.: Aspen Publishers, Inc., 1984.

Mundinger, M. *Home Care Controversy*. Rockville, Md.: Aspen Publishers, Inc., 1983.

National Association for Home Care. *A Proposal for Moving Towards a Prospective Payment System for Home Care*. Washington: National Association for Home Care, 1985.

National Association for Home Care. *Blueprint for Action: Toward a National Home Care Policy*. Washington: National Association for Home Care, 1986.

National League for Nursing. *Accreditation Criteria, Standards, and Substantiating Evidences*. New York: Accreditation Division for Home Care and Community Health, National League for Nursing, 1987.

Ott, M.J. "Quality Assurance: Monitoring Individual Compliance with Standards of Nursing Care." *Nursing Management* 18, no. 5 (1987): 57–64.

Pasquale, Debra K. "A Basis for Prospective Payment for Home Care." *Image: Journal of Nursing Scholarship* 19, no. 4 (1987): 186–191.

Pesznecker, B.L., and Paquin, R. "Implementing Interdisciplinary Team Practice in Home Care of Geriatric Clients." *Journal of Gerontologic Nursing* 8, no. 9 (1982): 504–508.

Peters, Donna Ambler, and Poe, Stephanie Storto. "Using Monitoring in a Home Care Quality Assurance Program." *Journal of Nursing Quality Assurance* 2, no. 3 (1988): 32–37.

Petersen, Mary Beth Harper. "Measuring Patient Satisfaction: Collecting Useful Data." *Journal of Nursing Quality Assurance* 2, no. 3 (1988): 25–35.

Phillips, E.K., and Cloonan, P.A. "DRG Ripple Effects on Community Health Nursing." *Public Health Nursing*, no. 2 (1987): 84–88.

Poe, Stephanie Storto, and Will, Janet Carney. "Quality Nurse-Patient Outcomes: A Framework for Nursing Practice." *Journal of Nursing Quality Assurance* 2, no. 1 (1987): 29–37.

Rinke, L.T. "Replacing a Failing Old Pattern with a Vital New Paradigm: Home Care." *Nursing and Healthcare* 8, no. 6 (1987): 331–333.

Rowe, J.W. "Health Care of the Elderly." *New England Journal of Medicine* 312 (1985): 827–836.

Saum, Margo F. "Evaluation: A Vital Component of the Quality Assurance Program." *Journal of Nursing Quality Assurance* 2, no. 4 (1988): 17–24.

Schmele, J.A. "A Method to Implement Nursing Standards in Home Health Care." *Journal of Nursing Quality Assurance* 1, no. 2 (1987): 43–52.

Schroeder, Patricia S., and Maibusch, Regina M., eds. *Nursing Quality Assurance: A Unit-Based*

*Approach.* Rockville, Md.: Aspen Publishers, Inc., 1984.

Smeltzer, Carolyn H. "Evaluating Program Effectiveness." In *Quality Assurance: A Complete Guide to Effective Programs*, edited by Claire G. Meisenheimer. Rockville, Md.: Aspen Publishers, Inc., 1985.

Smeltzer, Carolyn H. "Evaluating a Successful Quality Assurance Program: The Process." *Journal of Nursing Quality Assurance* 2, no. 4 (1988): 1–10.

Smeltzer, Carolyn H.; Feltman, Barbara; and Rajki, Karen. "Nursing Quality Assurance: A Process, Not a Tool." *Journal of Nursing Administration* 13, no. 1 (1983): 5–9.

Smith, N.K., and Meyer, A.B. "Personal Care Attendants: Key to Living Independently." *Rehabilitation Literature* 42 (1981): 258–265.

Smith Marker, Carolyn G. "Practical Tools for Quality Assurance: Criteria Development Sheet and Data Retrieval Form." *Journal of Nursing Quality Assurance* 2, no. 2 (1988): 43–54.

Swartzbeck, E. "The Problems of Falls in the Elderly." *Nursing Management* 14, no. 12 (1983): 34–38.

Sniff, David. "The Evolution of a Quality Assurance Program." *Quality Review Bulletin* 6 (1980): 27–30.

Tellis-Nayak, M. "The Challenge of the Nursing Role in the Rehabilitation of the Elderly Stroke Patient." *Nursing Clinics of North America* 21, no. 2 (1986): 339–343.

Thompson, Mary Wiles; Hylka, Sharon Canty; and Shaw, Carolyn Feltham. "Systematic Monitoring of Generic Standards of Patient Care." *Journal of Nursing Quality Assurance* 2, no. 2 (1988): 9–15.

Tinetti, M.; Williams, T.; and Mayewski, R. "Falls Risk Index for Elderly Patients Based on Number of Chronic Disabilities." *American Journal of Medicine*, 80 (March 1986): 429–434.

Vanaguras, A., et al. "Principles of Quality Assurance." *Quality Review Bulletin* 5, no. 2 (February 1979): 3–6.

Wagner, D.M. "Quality Assurance: Issues and Process." *Caring* 5, no. 9 (1986): 62–67.

Wagner, Peggy L. "Using a Questionnaire." In *Nursing Quality Assurance: A Unit-Based Approach*, edited by Patricia S. Schroeder and Regina M. Maibusch. Rockville, Md.: Aspen Publishers, Inc., 1984.

Wendorf, B. "Is Quality Assurance Really Worth It?" *Quality Review Bulletin* 7, no. 2 (1981): 23–28.

Whittaker, Alice, and McCanless, Lauri. "Nursing Peer Review: Monitoring the Appropriateness and Outcome of Nursing Care." *Journal of Nursing Quality Assurance* 2, no. 2 (1988): 24–31.

Wilbert, Catherine C. "Selecting Topics/Methodologies." In *Quality Assurance: A Complete Guide to Effective Programs*, edited by Claire G. Meisenheimer. Rockville, Md.: Aspen Publishers, Inc., 1985.

Wilson, Cathleen Krueger. "Program Evaluation: Theory, Method, and Practice." In *Nursing Quality Assurance: A Unit-Based Approach*, edited by Patricia S. Schroeder and Regina M. Maibusch. Rockville, Md.: Aspen Publishers, Inc., 1984.

Wilson, Cathleen Krueger. "Designing a Quality Assurance Program Evaluation: A Process Model." *Journal of Nursing Quality Assurance* 2, no. 4 (1988): 35–44.

Yeadon, Brenda E. "Assessing the Quality of Care in a Hospice Program." *Quality Review Bulletin* 13, no. 10 (October 1987): 336–339.

# Appendix 7-A

# Sample Nursing Quality Assurance Plan for Home Health Care

## PURPOSE

The division of nursing of _____ home health care provides home health nursing services to patients that are consistent with the objectives, goals, and mission of the agency. The nursing quality assurance program utilizes a planned, systematic, and ongoing process of monitoring and evaluating nursing practice and patient care in order to provide and improve the quality and appropriateness of patient care in the home setting.

## OBJECTIVES

- to evaluate nursing practice by the establishment of monitors and criteria for analysis of patient care based on nursing standards
- to identify trends, problems, or areas in nursing practice needing improvement
- to monitor the appropriateness, timeliness, and effectiveness of problem resolutions that impact on patient care and nursing practice.
- to improve communication and integration of activities with other disciplines in order to facilitate continuity and consistency in the provision of patient care
- to involve nursing personnel in quality assurance activities (i.e., monitoring, peer reviews, studies)

## AUTHORITY/PROGRAM ACCOUNTABILITY

The nursing administrator retains final authority and accountability for the implementation of nursing quality assurance activities. The administrator or a

179

designee functions as the chairperson of the nursing quality assurance committee and is the division's representative to the agencywide quality assurance committee. The chairperson is responsible for directing the nursing quality assurance program and ensuring the integration of information from monitoring and evaluating activities with other disciplines.

The nursing quality assurance committee includes representatives from the different nursing teams, shifts, and levels of the nursing staff. The committee is responsible for the planning and monitoring of quality assurance activities that evaluate the quality and appropriateness of patient care. The committee participates in the ongoing and systematic problem identification and resolution process. This includes the establishment of priorities for the problems that have an impact on the delivery of appropriate and effective patient care in order to improve the quality of nursing services. The nursing quality assurance committee meets on a monthly basis. Responsibilities of the committee include

- establishment of objective criteria to monitor and evaluate the standards of nursing care and the quality and appropriateness of nursing and patient care outcomes
- identification, compilation, and assessment of collected data and preparation of reports made to the nursing administrator, the agencywide quality assurance committee, and the agency administrator
- assessment of problems identified in patient care and evaluation of action taken to resolve the problems and improve care
- performance of annual review and revisions to the nursing quality assurance program
- annual review of the effectiveness of the monitoring, evaluation, and problem resolution process of the division of nursing
- documentation of all committee activities and committee meeting minutes
- integration of nursing quality assurance activities with other disciplines and that of the agencywide quality assurance committee, including total program evaluation and joint studies
- development/presentation of quarterly nursing quality assurance summaries to the agencywide quality assurance committee
- facilitation of nursing education to improve patient care

## IMPLEMENTATION

### Monitoring and Data Collection

Nursing practice is compared with standards of practice as established by the division of nursing. Development of standards is also based on the external standards of the National League for Nursing, National Homecaring Council, Joint Commission on Accreditation of Healthcare Organizations, American Nurses' Association, Commission on Accreditation of Rehabilitation Facilities, and the Association of Rehabilitation Nurses.

Monitors are established utilizing structure, process, and outcome standards. Criteria for acceptable/expected levels of practice are identified for each monitor (see Exhibit 7-A-1). Data for each monitor are collected and evaluated, and the results, including action taken, are reported to the nursing quality assurance committee (see Exhibit 7-A-2). Data collection is achieved through prospective, concurrent, and retrospective review, as appropriate. The sources of data, the person(s) responsible for the data collection, and the reporting frequency are established. Reports demonstrate the rate or percentage of occurrence and other information of interest derived from an analysis of the findings.

Specific sources of data collection include, but are not limited to

- nursing documentation
- adverse occurrence reports
- problem identification
- patient satisfaction surveys
- physician/staff concerns
- patient compliance
- safety and risk issues
- utilization review function
- medical record review
- nursing and agency administration
- communication from nursing and interdisciplinary team staff meetings
- evaluation of both staff development and patient/family education programs
- cost and availability of services
- results of surveys by outside organizations
- patient acuity
- patient classification system
- performance evaluations

## Problem Identification

Identified problems are resolved at the lowest level possible. Priority is established for problems that have an impact on the delivery and effectiveness of patient care. In establishing problem priority consider whether the problems

**Exhibit 7-A-1** Nursing Quality Assurance Monitors

| Standard | Monitor | Frequency of Data Collection | Expected Outcome Criteria | Method of Retrieval (Person[s] Responsible) |
|---|---|---|---|---|
| | | | | |

**Exhibit 7-A-2** Nursing Quality Assurance: Summary Report

| Monitor | Findings | Analysis | Action/Follow Up |
|---|---|---|---|
|  |  |  |  |

Month(s)/Year _____

Check:  _____ Monthly Summary
        _____ Quarterly Summary

- result in the delay/inappropriateness of care
- result from inconsistency in implementation of nursing practice based on standards, policies, procedures, and guidelines as established by the division of nursing
- have an impact on patient outcomes (e.g., program evaluation)
- involve a lengthy resolution
- involve other teams, disciplines, or services
- are isolated or recurring
- justify the time, effort, cost, and manpower needed to investigate and resolve them

The nursing quality assurance committee recommends action for problem resolution based on evaluation of collected data. Problems may be resolved by

- development of educational programs
- changes in existing resources (e.g., staffing patterns, supplies, equipment)
- reallocation of expenditures
- reassessment/revisions of goals, objectives, and standards of the division of nursing
- integration with other interdisciplinary team members
- counseling of personnel, including progressive disciplinary action

The resolution and corrective action should address the cause of the problem. In order to achieve an effective outcome, the plan of action should identify the expected change, who is responsible for effecting the change, the appropriate action (considering the severity and priority of the problem), and the anticipated time of resolution.

The effectiveness of problem resolution is documented and analyzed by the nursing quality assurance committee and is shared with the staff and nursing administration. Although the nursing administrator maintains responsibility for problem resolution and for evaluating the effectiveness of the corrective action, all nursing personnel are responsible for the delivery of quality nursing care, including problem identification and resolution.

## EVALUATION

Evaluation of the total nursing quality assurance program is performed annually by the nursing quality assurance committee. Revisions are made as necessary to ensure the continued provision of safe and appropriate patient care.

# Index

# About the Authors

ADRIANNE E. AVILLION, M.S., R.N., C.R.R.N., C.N.A., is the Rehabilitation Staff Development Specialist at Montebello Rehabilitation Hospital in Baltimore, Maryland. She has held a variety of staff development positions, including directing educational activities at a free-standing rehabilitation facility. She has published several articles on rehabilitation nursing and has presented papers at numerous local and national rehabilitation conferences.

BARBARA B. MIRGON, B.S.N., R.N., C.N.A., is the Quality Review Director at Montebello Rehabilitation Hospital in Baltimore, Maryland. Her professional experiences in rehabilitation have included the development and management of nursing and hospital quality assurance programs. She has given presentations on quality assurance issues in rehabilitation on the local and national level.